Saints' Names
for Confirmation

PAMELA HILL

THE VINEYARD PRESS
LONDON

The Vineyard Press
89a Winchester Street
Pimlico
London SW1V 4NU

1   3   5   7   9   10   8   6   4   2

Photoset in North Wales by
Derek Doyle & Associates, Mold, Clwyd.
Printed and bound in Great Britain by
WBC Book Manufacturers Limited,
Bridgend, Mid-Glamorgan.

Part
One

Names for Boys

Alban	Mark
Andrew	Martin
Anthony	Matthew
Benedict	Michael
Bernard	Nathaniel (Bartholomew)
Christopher	Nicholas
Daniel	Ninian
David	Oliver
Dominic	Patrick
Edward	Paul
Edmund	Peter
Francis	Philip, Philip Howard
George	Rupert
Hugh	Sebastian
James	Stephen
John, John Ogilvie	Thomas
Joseph	Timothy
Justin	Virgil
Luke	

Alban

You will certainly have heard of the town of St. Albans, and may have visited its great cathedral. If so, you will have seen the tomb of the protomartyr of Britain. Perhaps you also noticed on the wall – many people pass it by – a very old painting showing a burning fire and a severed head lying on the ground. It is sometimes stated that he was stoned or scourged first. The latter is more likely, as he was a Roman soldier.

This, his name and the fact of his death are all that are certainly known of Alban, but other things can be guessed at although, after so long a lapse of time – the year of his martyrdom was probably AD 209, though there is disagreement even about this – nothing can be proved. However, the presiding officer who ordered his death is said to have been Geta, the younger son of the emperor Septimius Severus. This makes the above date very probable, as there had been a rebellion in Britain in 207 and the emperor had come in person to suppress it. He marched to the extreme north of Scotland and on the way, lost 50,000 men through hardship, disease and the attacks of the men of Alban; note the name.

The Gaelic word for a Scot is still Albanach, and there were kings of Alban after the Romans left Britain two centuries later than the martyr's time. However, although it is possible that Albanus, as he would be called then, was a Scot, he could have come with the legions from any of the Roman provinces; Italy, Greece, Africa, Gaul, Germany and Spain are only a few. The

Roman empire had in fact grown so large that it was only possible to control it by using governors, or Caesars, appointed by the emperor, who of course continued to be called Caesar himself and to retain central control. He did not, by then, always live in Rome, nor was he always a Roman except by citizenship. Septimius Severus was himself an African by birth; before him, the earlier Hadrian, who also visited Britain and built a great wall to keep out the Scots, was born in Spain.

Most of the wall built by Hadrian can still be seen, and we know something of the life lived by the garrisons who manned it. Slightly further north, there was a wall of which very little trace remains. It stretched between the Forth and the Clyde, and is still remembered as Antonine's Wall, although Septimius Severus repaired it on his visit. Living there, in the same manner as on Hadrian's Wall further south, would be legionaries and their families, some of whom may well have been Christian. This is probable because the emperor Antonine, who lived from AD86 to 161, had tolerated Christianity and had forbidden persecutions, which had been the rule under the first emperors such as Nero. Antoninus Pius, as he is called, was not himself a Christian, but he was a kindly man, and it would have been possible for a Roman legionary manning the northernmost wall to bring up his family in the Christian faith. However, the arrival of Severus changed all that; Severus had already done to death many Christians in Carthage and Rome, chiefly at the marriage celebrations of his elder son Caracalla. The younger, Geta, was anxious to please his father on the British visit and prove the efficiency of his own command. In other words, it was by then dangerous to be a Christian in the Roman army and to say so.

Meantime, Septimius Severus had abolished the old Praetorian guard and, instead, picked legionaries as his guards, bringing them from wherever they might have been posted. It is therefore at least probable that the soldier Alban was brought down to the settlement then known as Verulamium and carried out his duties there. There could of course have been other origins of his name.

Alba Longa (it is now Castel Gandolfo) was the first town built by the early Romans; thirteen miles to the south-east of Rome is a Lake Albanus; there is Albania, also a town named Alba Iulia in Romania, and Alban in France in the Tarn mountains, near the town of Albi. Britain itself is known as Albion; but one cannot help remembering the lost wall built by kindly Antonine and the freedom with which Christian legionaries might live there and rear sons to follow them in the Roman army, the finest available career. It could not only take a man to foreign places; it could earn him promotion to become governor or even emperor. Several of these, including Septimius himself, had started as mere soldiers.

We will never know one way or the other about that, but the second mystery surrounding Alban is the supposed manner of his arrest. It is usually given out that he saved the life of his friend Amphibilus, who was a priest, by donning his cloak to allow his escape. When the guards came to take the priest, Alban threw off the cloak, saying 'It is I, Alban, and I will die for Christ'. While conversions can be as sudden, the fact remains that the name Amphibilus is stated, itself, to mean cloak: in other words, either the name of Alban's priest friend is unknown, or there is more to it. On looking up a Latin dictionary, I found that the words for 'cloak' were *lacerna, sagum,* and *pallium*. There was no word given as *amphibilus*, though it may exist in larger dictionaries. There was however a word *amphibolia*, which means 'ambiguity'.

Look up your own dictionary and see how this last word is explained. Mine says it means 'double meaning' or 'having more than one meaning'. In other words, it is a mystery. Alban died for a veiled mystery. What could this have been except the Host itself? In other words, Alban was already a Christian. He had possibly been in the habit of finding out where Mass was said, doubtless in the place where by tradition he was arrested, a secret spot among trees near a river, within riding distance of Verulamium, now St. Albans. The secret chantry can still be visited if one obtains the key. Its foundations were uncovered this century by the nuns then living at All Saints' Centre, London Colney. They removed the earth which had covered them and placed a stone altar on the spot. There is a centuries-old tradition that this is where St. Alban was taken.

He was tried before Geta, who hesitated to lose a good soldier and suggested that if he would worship Caesar, namely his father, all would be overlooked. However, Alban refused steadily, and unwilling to risk a rebuke from the emperor when he should return from the north (in fact Septimius Severus died at York within two years) Geta ordered his execution, possibly also scourging as Christ had endured it, with metal-tipped thongs. The executioner, a fellow-officer, refused to carry out his orders and a substitute had to be found; but the thing was done. There is a statue of a young Roman soldier, holding up the Host, in the chapel at All Saints', about a mile from the chantry; and from the office there, one can ask for the key. The saint's feast day is 22nd June, a pleasant time to walk through the summer woods and remember St. Alban.

Andrew

Andrew was the first of the disciples to notice Jesus. It happened when he and his brother Simon, later known as Peter, had journeyed to the banks of the Jordan from Capernaum, where they were fishermen, although their birthplace was in Bethsaida, a nearby town further from the lake.

They had gone to hear the strange prophet John the Baptist preach repentance and to watch him baptise in the river. This time, he said of one of those who had been baptised 'Behold the Lamb of God'.

Andrew saw at once that there was something about this other man which even the Baptist did not possess. He determined to follow him and find out more, but first he sought out his brother Simon in the crowd and persuaded him to come. 'We have found the Messiah,' he said (John 1, 42.) The Messiah was the one who was expected by all Israel; it had also been the name used by the anointed kings of Israel. It was a downright statement for a fisherman to make.

The brothers followed the way Jesus had gone and shortly saw him walking ahead. As he always did, he knew they had come to seek him out. He turned round. 'What do you want of me?' he said. The brothers replied that they wanted to learn more of him; where did he live? 'Come and see,' Jesus said. We do not know where he took them. It cannot have been to his home at Nazareth, which was too far away. He talked to them all day, and then they went back to Capernaum.

When they saw him again, John the Baptist had been arrested and put in prison. Jesus walked past the lakeside, where the two brothers had put out their boat into the water and were casting their nets, while their partners John and James were mending theirs on shore. 'Follow me, and I will make you fishers of men,' Jesus said this time. Having heard him talk earlier, they left their nets (and their livelihood) and followed. It must be remembered that it was not the first time they had met Jesus, and that they had heard what John the Baptist had to say of him. The story is often told as if a complete stranger had walked past and had beckoned them, but they had had time to think about Jesus and to remember the other things he had said at the earlier meeting, in the place where he was living, wherever that was. We do not know if James and John had previous knowledge of the kind, but they followed also.

Thereafter they became aware of the fame Jesus was acquiring in Galilee, in something the same way as the Baptist had already done; but the Baptist had not cast out devils, as Jesus did soon in the synagogue in Andrew's presence. Moreover there was the cure of Simon's mother-in-law, who had a fever in the little house they all shared in Capernaum, near the shore.

The next mention of Andrew is when he, or another disciple, admired the splendour of the Temple in Jerusalem, which was by far the most magnificent building the Bethsaida fishermen could ever have seen. Jesus sadly foretold how it would be destroyed, with not a stone left standing. Later, in a private place he loved on the Mount of Olives, Andrew and the rest questioned him more closely; and were told a great deal more, including what would become of themselves for supporting him; they would be flogged and cast out of the synagogues, and handed over to die. They were told of the other things that would happen, the earthquakes and the darkening of sun and moon, and the falling of stars from the sky when the Son of Man should come on clouds of glory; and to be on guard constantly and to pray. There must have been a great deal of this which made them afraid, but they stayed with Jesus even when many others left him.

It was Andrew who noticed, later on at Tabgha, the place of green grass, that there was a boy with five loaves and two fish, but what good was that among so many? We know what happened, and that miracle must have gone even further to convince the brothers that here was indeed the Son of Man, the one who was to redeem Israel.

There was another disciple named Philip, whom the brothers had also known in Bethsaida. Perhaps for this reason it was to Andrew that Philip brought certain Greeks, or possibly Andrew himself spoke some Greek; probably Jesus did. The outcome then was the story of the grain of wheat, which must fall into the ground and die if it is to bear fruit. At this point thunder was heard by the listening crowd. The signs were becoming more ominous.

Andrew is not mentioned again until after the Crucifixion. He was in the upper room with Christ's mother and the disciples when the fire of Pentecost came down. Like the rest he received the gift of tongues, and later on we know he preached in Greece and was martyred in Scythia. He asked to be crucified on a cross placed cornerways, a saltire. In an old hymn he is made to say in Scots, as he became the patron saint of Scotland, 'O couthie cross!' The word couthie is difficult to translate; it can mean comfortable, welcome, friendly. Andrew died on it, and at Patras, in the Peloponnese, his head is preserved in a reliquary. It shows the face of a man who has been dead for almost two thousand years. The face is still pleasant.

Anthony

There are two famous saints called Anthony; do not confuse them as they are quite different. One was St. Anthony of Egypt, a very early saint who despite living as a hermit in the desert, died aged 104 years if the records are accurate! He is the St. Anthony of the Temptations and also, the saint who used to be prayed to for cures of erysipelas, a severe and painful skin rash known as St. Anthony's Fire. He also began the monastic movement by his example. However our St. Anthony of Padua lived much later and in these times, is much more often remembered, and more familiar to us.

He was not born in Padua, but in Lisbon in 1195. It is like him to be thought of in two places, as in his lifetime he was often seen in places so far apart it could not be imagined how he had got to them both at almost the same time. It is certainly true that he travelled great distances, but it is also possible that he had the gift of bilocation, as it is called. He was able to do a great many things ordinary people cannot; he was said to be able to walk on water, like Christ. This is possible; certain others have done it. Like Christ also, St. Anthony was still a young man when he died.

Anthony

His parents were noble, which meant that as a boy in Portugal he received a good education which would have been denied to a peasant. This was to stand him in good stead when he came to teach others. Meantime, when he was 15 years old he joined the Canons Regular of São Vicente in Lisbon, his home. After two years there he progressed to the study house of the Augustinian Canons at Santa Cruz in Coimbra. This is a place further north on the same coast, still in view of the sea but with mountains behind. There Anthony became proficient in Scripture, but he was disappointed by the everlasting patronage of the Court, which he thought should not interfere with the life of the cloister. He was not interested in place-seeking.

About then, he heard certain news which influenced him to exchange the cloister for the world. It was not long since the Franciscan order had been founded, and its friars went out into town streets to preach, having taken a vow of poverty. They were unafraid of disease or danger, and soon became missionaries in lands which were not Christian. Several of these good and harmless brothers were martyred in Morocco, and when Anthony, in his sheltered cloister, heard this, he decided to abandon his scholarly and secluded life and join the Franciscan Order. It was a tremendous decision to make and must have shocked his fellow-canons. However despite their pleas to him to remain, he left and donned the grey habit. There was already a friary in Coimbra, and it may not be coincidence that its name was San Antonio.

Anthony soon asked to be sent to Morocco, where the friars had met their deaths. Permission was given, but he was not a strong man physically. Illness forced him to return, much against his will. However results were to prove that it was the will of God. His boat was driven off course by storms, and he landed in Sicily. Nobody knew him there and he knew nobody, and at first could not speak the tongue. However he knew Latin, and soon learned Italian, which is not very different from Spanish and Portuguese. Anthony was in fact so quick at learning languages that he was soon able to take an active part in a Chapter, a great meeting of the Order, at Portiuncula in 1221. Although still only twenty-six, he was sent to be in charge of the Franciscan province of the Romagna, a marshy district near Rome itself. This cannot have been good for his health, but he considered that so little that he taxed himself further with penances endured in solitude at the hermitage of Monte Paolo, near Forlì. This is another marshy place, between Ravenna and Rimini. It is almost as though Anthony sought out the places that were worst for him; fevers abounded in these low-lying places, though here there was the sight, again, of the sea.

Having been ordained, he was commanded to preach against heresy in North Italy. He did this for the next two years, then was transferred to the South of France. In this quite different country a terrible heresy had taken root, despite the legend that long before, St. Mary Magdalene had come there and had made many conversions. The sect against whom Anthony was to set his wits was known as the Albigensian one, because it was rife in a town named Albi although before that, it had spread from the Balkans. Its beliefs had spread not only to southern France but to Italy, Germany and Flanders. The Albigenses believed that good and evil are equally eternal, a depressing thought. They did not allow their followers to have children. They denied the Incarnation, Passion and Resurrection of Our Lord. They thought of themselves as highly moral – such people always do – but it can be seen that their beliefs greatly alarmed the Pope, Innocent III, a little later; enough to make him declare a crusade against them as was done against the Saracens. This lasted twenty years, until only a very few of the sect were left alive and fled to Piedmont. By that time, Anthony himself was long dead.

He had preached all over Italy by then for three years, daily in Padua in Lent of 1231, the year he died. Crowds thronged to hear his preaching, and it was then that many legends arose round him; it was said he had a silver tongue.

Francis of Assisi, his director, had already appointed him to become the first professor of theology to the friars. This was of great importance, as it proved that poverty need not be accompanied by ignorance. Many who had mocked at the poor friars soon found that they were as well able to answer questions on theology as any learned doctor in the universities.

Anthony did not however content himself with this demanding task, which would have been more than enough for most people. He became also Guardian of Le Puy, *custos* of Limoges, Provincial of the Romagna. Look at the map and see how far apart all those places are, think of the difficulty of travel in those days, and ask yourself how Anthony managed to get to all of them without bilocation! There were also miracles reported of him; the famous one of the fish that swarmed inshore to hear him preach, and the hungry mule that knelt before the Host when he asked it, thereby converting its master. Like St. Francis, Anthony had what is known as rapport with animals. He is the patron of the lower kinds, St. Francis of the upper.

Anthony died in the year of his unforgotten Lenten preaching in Padua, and was canonised only a year later, on 30th May 1232. Pope Gregory IX described him as 'a teacher of the Church.' Much later, in 1946, Pope Pius XII named him Doctor Evangelicus, a high honour which places him beside St. Thomas Aquinas and St. Bernard of Clairvaux.

It is not certain what he looked like. A portrait painted more than a hundred years after his death, in Santa Croce in Florence, shows a man who looks much older than thirty-six, with a face puffy with ill-health. The likeness may however have been taken from an earlier one or described by someone who knew someone who remembered Anthony. I found a little wooden statue in the Santo Spirito arcades in Rome, showing the saint as a slender young man, tonsured and wearing his Franciscan habit and rope girdle. He is often portrayed as carrying the Christ Child, who it is said appeared to him; or sometimes with lilies, a book, a cross, or a flame, or burning heart, long before the Sacred Heart devotion. Time and place seem to have been overcome by him;

he remains near us, and answers prayer at once, often with a leg-pull. He finds lost objects like keys, and often makes one find the wrong key first! He is invoked both for spiritual and bodily needs; he is the patron saint of lovers, of marriages and births, of obsession, fevers, diseases of animals, and the post. Letters are much more likely to get there if one says 'St. Anthony guide'. He also protects miners. His missionaries, the White Fathers, do wonderful work in Africa and in educating boys to become priests, or merely educating them.

Charity is his speciality, and St. Anthony's Bread for the poor has a box in every church. Since last century there has been a Prayer League dedicated to him, also the Tuesday devotion, as he was buried on a Tuesday, June 17th 1231.

Amazingly also, almost four centuries after his death he was made an admiral twice over! The first time it was for helping the Portuguese, his fellow-countrymen, to win a victory at sea over the French in 1710. The second time was in 1732, when he helped the Spanish to expel the Moors from Oran in North Africa. It is almost as though he remembered the Franciscan martyrs of Morocco and his own wish to replace them in his lifetime. However, much as he did then, he has done even more since his death. He is a constant reminder that this is not the only world, and that when we die we continue to be ourselves. Somebody who unfailingly answers in small things is a help in great ones. *St. Antoine de Padoue, priez pour nous.* He is not forgotten in France.

Benedict

St. Benedict was born in 480 and died in 543, so he was not the very old man with a long white beard depicted in a famous painting. He was born of a well-to-do family at Nursia, near Spoleto. It was a time of change for the known world, as the Roman Empire, which had ruled everywhere for centuries, was invaded by barbarians and nothing seemed certain any more.

Benedict knew that he wanted to be out of the world, at first alone. It must be remembered that in those days there were no monastic communities; it was Benedict who thought of them. Meantime he reflected and prayed in a cave at Subiaco. (There is a suburb of this name now in Perth, Western Australia.)

He became known for his life of prayer, and was made abbot of Vicovaro, which might be called an experimental monastery. Benedict found the life too lax, and left with a few followers. They were the sons of rich Romans and even a few Goths, barbarian people who were beginning to acquire knowledge after the first invasions.

By the end, Benedict had founded 12 monasteries, and had written out the first book of rules for monastic living, the *Regula Monachorum*. In 529, he and his black-robed monks founded the famous monastery of Monte Cassino, near Naples. Benedictine monasteries are always built on hills, and as time passed this one became filled with rare and precious books and treasures. Sadly, it was a target in the Second World War.

Before he died St. Benedict had advanced the state of education, medicine, prayer and the liturgy. He also faced the king of the Goths, named Totila, and reproached him for the destruction of Christianised Rome. Benedict's sister, Scholastica, also a saint, helped him in the founding of a rule for women. It is said that rain fell when she prayed for it.

Over the centuries, though the Benedictine order did great things including the conversion of England from 597, they themselves became a trifle lax – this happens with any long-established order – and saints such as Anthony of Padua and Bernard of Clairvaux took other ways of manifesting holiness and the desire for a community life. At the present day the Benedictine order is famous for education at schools like

Ampleforth, and for contributing to the glory of God in music and rich ceremonies. They also make a very famous liqueur!

Bernard

Bernard of Clairvaux, as he is always known, was born in 1090 near Dijon. His father's name was Tescelin, his mother's Aletta. He had five brothers and a sister.

He went to study under the secular canons at St. Vorles, but they do not seem to have taught him the classics. Nevertheless Bernard was always able to express himself in clear, fluent and polished words, whether in speaking or writing.

When he was 17 his mother, to whom he had been devoted, died. Bernard then retired from the world at Châtillon. His five brothers were persuaded to join him in religion, but his sister refused and instead, chose to marry. This angered Bernard – he was easily made angry by those who disagreed with him – and when his sister travelled a long way to visit him, refused to receive her. This shows a side of his nature at odds with the one he professed, namely that God made man out of love and redeemed him out of love. Bernard was harsh also with scholars who disagreed with him. One of these was the penitent Abélard.

Bernard criticised the lax standards into which he said the Benedictine order had fallen. Instead, the Cistercian discipline, which he kept, was the strictest in Europe. After only three years he was elected abbot. With 12 companions, after the manner of Christ, he founded the monastery of Clara Vallis, Clairvaux, in the valley of the Aube. Cistercian monasteries are always in valleys, near clear running water.

Before he died Bernard had founded 68 abbeys, though he himself seldom left Clairvaux. He had a profound effect on the thought of his time. His dispute with Abbot Peter of Cluny, a Benedictine foundation, began in 1119. However he and the Abbot managed to remain friends, it is said, out of mutual charity.

It was perhaps Bernard's own rich interior life of the spirit that made him impatient of disagreement. He is said to have had great and persuasive charm, and young men of the time were widely influenced by him, especially as the *Gestes of Arthur* had been circulated about then, with the ideal of Galahad, the knight of pure life. The thought of Clairvaux coincided with the rise of the age of chivalry.

Some of Bernard's convictions are not perhaps ours as taught today; for instance he refused to believe in the Immaculate Conception of Our Lady although he was devoted to her, and accepted the Assumption. On the other hand his ideas about baptism are modern; he believed it could happen with blood as much as with water, also by desire; and that unbaptised infants could be redeemed by the faith of their parents.

Abélard's condemnation took place in 1140, and six years later Bernard preached the Second Crusade at Vézelay in Burgundy. The enthusiasm of the crowds was such that fragments were torn from his cloak to make crosses to pin on their shoulders. The crusade ended in failure, which saddened Bernard towards the end of his life.

He died, worn out with austerities, in 1153, at Clairvaux. He was canonised 21 years later by Pope Alexander III; declared a Doctor of the Church in 1830, and 'mellifluous doctor' by Pope Pius XII, just before your time.

There are many other saints of the name of Bernard; one of Cluny, the place of argument, wrote bitter poetry which has been compared to Dante's.

Christopher

'St. Christopher has been declared redundant', somebody said to me not long ago. This is a pity, as there are two of them.

Until recently, drivers of cars often carried a small round medal, often of blue enamel and sometimes built into the dashboard, of a giant carrying the Christ Child on his shoulder. He was therefore supposed to be a protection to travellers. The story is that the little child appeared and asked the giant to carry him across a deep river. The giant did so, but as he made his way through the water the burden he was carrying grew heavier and heavier, so that in the end it seemed as if he was bearing the weight of the whole world. Afterwards the giant was called Christopher, which means Christ-bearer.

Many threads go to make up the tapestry of this tale. One is of Atlas, a giant who bore the weight of the world on his shoulders. A race of giants certainly lived in the world at one time. We sometimes see or hear of one today, but that is usually because of an overactive gland deep in the brain, called the pituitary, which can cause overgrowth of the bones. Such giants do not as a rule live to old age. The early race of giants was however strong. Their bones have been found in Menton, in the south of France. This is not so astonishing; the earth was once peopled with giant snails, and giant dogs' bones have been dug up on the island of Gran Canaria, hence its name (from *canis*, nothing to do with canaries).

Early Greek legends tell of the war between the Titans, who were giants, and the newer gods, who conquered them. Another tradition is that the entire race of giants was drowned in the Flood. Certainly there were two famous ones, Gog and Magog, who are mentioned in Genesis, Ezekiel and the Book of Revelation, and there is Gogmagog Hill near Cambridge, also many older people remember the two giants' images which used to be in the old London Guildhall, destroyed in the Second World War. Ulysses, on his travels, met the giant Polyphemus, who had a single eye in the middle of his forehead. (This may have been his pituitary).

The giant called Christopher is therefore not an impossibility, though his race had died out long before the time of Christ. It is however probable that a very old pagan folk memory interferes here.

If you look at the ordnance map, you will see on the way to Swindon in Wiltshire, near the Whitehorse Hill, a place named Wayland's Smithy. Wayland was not a giant, but in his youth had been a handsome young man, and such a clever goldsmith that he could make the finest swords and jewels in the world. He was captured by a king who was his enemy, and hamstrung, which means that the tendons behind his knees were cut so that he could only crouch and creep. The king put him on an island and told him to make swords. Instead, Wayland invented a pair of wings so that he could fly wherever he liked. There are many stories about him, some lost; but one tells of how he carried his little son Widia on his shoulder across a stretch of water nine yards deep. Compare this with the St. Christopher story, and remember how the Christian Church used pagan tales and feast days to change to their own, like 25th December, which used to be the festival of the sun and fire. It made a missionary's task easier to use what the pagans already understood.

The second St. Christopher perhaps deserves to be better known than the first, which is perhaps one reason why the Church took the giant out of the calendar and replaced him with St. Frances of Rome for travellers, as she travelled a great deal. The second Christopher was martyred in Syria in the 3rd century, and he has a feast day in both the Roman and Greek Churches; the first is July 25th, the second May 9th. His miracles made the prefect Dagnus alarmed, because the emperor in Rome, Decius, was extremely hard on Christians and persecuted them if found. Dagnus reported the miracles to Rome, and the emperor sent back word that Christopher was to be shot with poisoned arrows. This was attempted, but the arrows rebounded and instead, wounded Dagnus, who began to writhe in agony. Christopher therefore 'suffered himself to be beheaded, that his blood might heal his enemy.' To us this may seem like taking forgiveness a little far! – but the *Golden Legend*, written in 1483 from older sources, relates the tale.

In any case, and whatever happened or did not, a great many people still carry a St. Christopher medal in their cars. You have chosen a good name, whether you are thinking of the giant or of the martyr.

Daniel

There are at least three Daniels worth mention. To take them in order, the first is the prophet from the Book of Daniel in the Old Testament, who was taken as a boy from Jerusalem to Babylon with three others. The four were chosen by the king as being worth educating, and among other things they learned the language and secrets of the Chaldeans. However they did not forsake their own religion, and when the king sent meat and wine daily, refused it. The king, who was easily made angry – his name was Nebuchadnezzar – threatened the boys with punishment. Daniel, who had a cool head, asked for three days to live with his friends on pulses and water instead. At the end of the three days the Jewish captives looked in much better health than anyone else, and the king began to notice Daniel as a wise lad. Shortly Nebuchadnezzar had a dream, and rather unreasonably he sent for his wise men and told them to interpret the dream, but refused to tell them what it was, and said that if they could not do as he asked their lives would be forefeit and their goods thrown on a dunghill.

This terrified them, and somebody remembered Daniel. He prayed a great deal, and this time asked God to tell him what the king's dream had been and to help him interpret it. It is rather like the story of Joseph. God told Daniel the dream had been of a great idol, made of gold at its head, silver in its body, and iron and clay at its feet. It was to be interpreted as meaning that all the glory of Babylon would topple because of the feet of clay.

Daniel put this very courteously to the king. Instead of killing him, which might have happened, Nebuchadnezzar gave him promotion and he became an important person about court. Later the king had a second dream, which Daniel also interpreted, and this foretold the king's madness; he ended in a field eating grass. You can read all about it in the Book of Daniel, which is quite short.

Nebuchadnezzar's son Belshazzar became king, and offended God by holding a great feast in which the vessels of gold and silver were used which had been taken from the Temple in Jerusalem. A hand appeared, and wrote certain words on the wall which no one understood. Again, Daniel was sent for. He told the king that he would die.

This happened, and Darius the Mede became king of Babylon. Darius was a pleasanter man than Belshazzar, and grew fond of Daniel, who by then was no longer a boy. He wanted to give so wise a man full power in his new kingdom, in something the same way as Pharaoh had given it to Joseph. However Daniel was said to have destroyed the idol of the god Bel and a dragon sacred to the Babylonians, and in any case there was envy of him among the other courtiers. Against his will, the king was forced to throw Daniel into a deep pit where lions were, and to seal the entrance stone. He spent a sleepless night, and in the morning went and called Daniel's name, expecting him to be dead. However Daniel answered cheerfully, and when the stone was moved walked out of the lions' den unharmed. Lions in fact are respecters of persons and probably knew Daniel was not afraid of them. When the wicked courtiers were thrown to them instead, they broke their bones to pieces at once.

Daniel was granted apocalyptic visions, like prophets before and after him. He mentions the Son of God, and his friends Shadrach, Mesach and Abed-Nego were at one point put into a fiery furnace for refusing to worship a golden idol one of the kings had erected. They were seen to walk unharmed in the midst of the fire, and a fourth was seen walking with them 'like the Son of God.' Although it is certainly not beyond the power of God to pass certain people through fire unharmed, it is possible that this story is what is called an allegory, representing the resurrection of the dead.

The other Daniel was a Franciscan, St. Daniel of Belvedere, martyred at Ceuta, North Africa, in 1227. He was the provincial of Calabria, and had asked to go out to the mission despite earlier massacres there. On the night before he and his brother friars went out to preach, they confessed and received Communion, and had the ceremony of the washing of feet. On Sunday, 3rd October, they preached after the manner of St. Francis, relying on the Holy Spirit, though they knew no Arabic. They were taken and imprisoned as fools, and eight days later beheaded for having refused to renounce their faith. The Christians in the town were allowed to bury them.

An Abbot Daniel had come from Russia to the Holy Land in 1122, at a time when the Greek and Latin branches of the Church were in full agreement. He became Bishop of Tartu in Estonia, and died there after writing the story of his pilgrimage.

David

St. David, the patron saint of Wales, was born at St. Bride's Bay, now in Pembroke, in 520 or earlier. He lived till 589, and his feast day is 1st March.

He did not, like some others, come to a pagan country. The Welsh were Celts, and the Celtic races had fled westwards to the mountains at the coming of the pagan Saxons to what was later England. The Celts took with them Christianity, which had existed among them from the days of the late Roman Empire, a generation before. David – Dewi in Welsh – was able to study under St. Paulinus of Wales and later to travel as a missionary, also to visit the Holy Land. He was consecrated archbishop by the Patriarch of Jerusalem.

Like many Welshmen today, he was known for his silences. He mortified himself greatly and was an incessant worker. He was known as 'Aquaticus' because he drank only water. He preached against Pelagianism, a heresy which has a certain amount of reason about it, but while David preached at Brefi a hill rose under his feet and a dove came to perch on his shoulder.

'Be joyful and keep the faith. Do those little things you have seen and heard from me,' is the message he left. He was canonised in 1120. More than 50 churches are named after him in Wales.

There was a king of Scots named David the Saint, but he was merely the son of one, St. Margaret. He built nine glorious abbeys in Scotland, mostly along the Border: their ruins can still be seen. He died in 1153, and a much later king, James VI, referred to him wryly as 'a sair sanct to the croun' because of the money spent on the abbeys. This is how the name arose.

The most famous David of all is of course the shepherd boy, son of Jesse, who was secretly anointed king of Israel by the prophet Samuel in place of Saul. David often played his harp to cheer Saul, who was given to depressive moods. However war broke out between them despite David's great friendship with Saul's son Jonathan. When Saul and Jonathan were killed at last in battle David grieved for them, although he himself had had years of rough living as a kind of guerilla fighter owing to the enmity of Saul. David grieved also later for his own rebellious son Absalom. He loved greatly, and his love for Bathsheba, who became his wife, caused him to have her first husband Uriah killed in the front line of battle. As a result, God caused the death of their first child. A second became Solomon, known in time for his wisdom. Meantime David reigned for almost forty years. He wrote some, though not all, of the Psalms; perhaps the one most likely to be his is *The Lord is my shepherd*. 'Hosanna to the Son of David' shows how greatly David's memory was honoured even by the time of Christ, when riding in triumph into Jerusalem, which David had made his capital, though he was not considered worthy to build the Temple there and it was built by his son. His own city, Bethlehem, is where Christ chose to be born. 'Once in royal David's city' is a favourite carol of ours.

Dominic

If anyone is asked what St. Dominic was like, they probably do not know. If they are asked about St. Francis, they know at once. Yet the two saints lived more or less at the same time, and were trying, more or less, to do the same thing; in other words, to bring Christ into ordinary people's lives by living like the apostles, going about and preaching openly, owning nothing and relying on alms. It is what Christ told his disciples to do on their first journey without him, and if you remember they came back surprised at the things they had been able to do on the journey without any luggage.

Dominic and Francis however differed in detail, at least at the outset. Francis did not think learning was necessary for his friars at first, though later he came to see that they ought to know enough to answer questions. Dominic knew this at the beginning. In all the houses of his Order of Preachers there was, from the start, a lecturer in theology. It is interesting to know that the first of these was an Englishman, Alexander Stevensby.

Two things are remembered about St. Dominic by those outside his Order. One is that he preached, as did St. Francis and St. Anthony, during the Albigensian crusade. This was a war declared by Pope Innocent III against a heretical sect who had murdered a papal legate. Long before that they had been troublesome, and their presence, mostly in France, was the chief reason for the existence of the friars, who preached outside monasteries. They had so much success that it is said 150 people were converted in one day by a sermon of St. Dominic. On another occasion he sat up all night to convert an Albigensian innkeeper, and managed it. On the whole, however, the sect was very stubborn and very dangerous, believing among other things that the world was made by evil instead of by God. They dressed simply and went about the towns to try to show, by their example, how much better they were than the monks who shut themselves away in monasteries, or the rich bishops, or the Pope. The appearance of the friars, likewise dressed simply, and preaching that the world was made by a God who loved us so much that he sent his only son to be our sacrifice, did as much to defeat the Albigenses as the war waged on them by the Pope and the king of France, details of which are very cruel.

The other thing to remember about St. Dominic is the vision he had of Our Lady, who instructed him in the mysteries of the rosary. Nowadays it seems to us a little unnecessary unless we are devoted to it, which many people are. It has to be remembered that in Dominic's time, poor people could not read, had no light after sunset, were often ignorant of the facts of the Catholic Faith, and could almost teach themselves in the darkness by counting the beads, reciting the mysteries, or, if they had no beads, using their fingers. It was a timely instruction at a difficult time for the Church, exactly as the Lourdes apparitions were to be, many centuries after.

St. Dominic was a very humble man, although his birth is said to have been aristocratic. He offered, at the second General Chapter of his Order, to resign, as he did not want to be placed more highly than his brothers; he had asked to be buried at their feet. They would not accept his resignation, but he died shortly after. He is said to answer prayer marvellously. His belief that service to God can be stifled by too much spiritual security, as well as by too much material security, is food for thought today as much as in his lifetime. He was canonised in 1234, thirteen years after his death. He had sent members of his Order to all seats of learning, including Oxford where they still are.

There is one more charming legend about St. Dominic which you may like to remember. Before he was born, his mother, who was a very pious woman, had a dream of a black-and-white dog holding a lighted candle in its mouth. As Dominican friars adopted the black habit of the Augustinians, and wear a white robe beneath, they remembered this story and call themselves *domini canes*, the dogs of God. The Latin language is full of puns.

Edward

To understand the story of St. Edward the Confessor, it is necessary to know something about his family.

His grandfather was King Edgar, a descendant of Alfred the

Great. Alfred's memory was greatly honoured by the English, as he had saved them from the Danes and had, probably, saved Christianity in this country. You may know Chesterton's poem which ends *When Wessex went to battle for the Creed*.

King Edgar married twice, and when he died his elder son Edward inherited. This young man is known as Edward the Martyr. He was murdered by his stepmother in the presence of her own son Ethelred, aged ten. Ethelred was then made king in his half-brother's place.

It was a bad start, and Ethelred grew up into the kind of man who can never make decisions. By that time, England was again in constant danger from Danish raids. Although Alfred had forced them at the time to accept Christianity, they were so far from it now that they killed an archbishop of Canterbury by throwing meat-bones at him after a feast.

King Ethelred made the mistake of trying to buy them off with money. Of course they only came back for more. At last, in 1002, the year of his own second marriage to the duke of Normandy's daughter Emma, the king ordered a huge massacre of Danes, including women and children. Among the murdered women was the sister of Sweyn, the Danish leader.

Naturally war followed, and at one point Ethelred and his wife Emma, with their two sons Alfred and Edward, had to flee across the Channel to Normandy. It is important to remember this, as it was the place where Edward was brought up, and the language he spoke was French.

Ethelred was able to return to England later, and his son by a first marriage, Edmund Ironside, fought Cnut, the son of Sweyn, and for a short time divided England up with him. However Edmund Ironside died by treachery, and Ethelred himself died at almost the same time. Cnut the Dane not only became king of all England, but married Ethelred's Norman widow Emma. Cnut made not a bad king, and professed Christianity, even making a journey to Rome to visit the Pope. He and Emma had a son, Harthacnut, who became king on his father's death.

However Harthacnut drank far too much to be likely to live long, and Edward, still in Normandy, was called back to England by the influence of a powerful noble, Godwin of Wessex. Godwin had already murdered Edward's brother Alfred the Atheling (this word means heir). He himself had many sons, and as it was known that Edward had taken a vow of chastity, thought that by the end his own family would inherit. He made sure of this by forcing Edward to marry his daughter Edith.

Edith was beautiful and pious, but it is understandable that Edward was reluctant for the marriage. He became king in 1042, and he and Edith were married three years later. Meantime, Earl Godwin was seated at the high table with the king. Edward accused him of his brother Alfred's murder. 'May this bread choke me if it was so,' said Godwin. The bread did choke him, and he died.

King Edward became known as the Confessor (accent on the first syllable). His life was saintly and his laws just. He was much beloved, and dispensed charity to the sick and poor. He had a long reign in peace, which made the English look back on it afterwards with regret. Edward built a church he called the West Minster, and dedicated it to St. Peter. Rebuilt in a later reign, we know it now as Westminster Abbey.

Edward's court was full of Normans, and it is probable that his mother's great-nephew, William Duke of Normandy, visited him and obtained a promise that, as Edward had no heirs, he would inherit the crown. This is not certain, and when the king was dying he named his queen's brother, Godwin's son Harold, as his successor. The English would greatly have preferred a Saxon king, but as we know, William of Normandy had other ideas. He defeated and killed Harold at Hastings in the very year King Edward had died, 1066.

Edward was buried in his church of the West Minster. We know what it was like from the Bayeux Tapestry, which also shows his death. As it was probably not completed till about 1150, this proves in what respect Edward's memory was held by the people of England and even of Normandy. The church is shown with round arches, in the early fashion.

King Edward was probably an albino, which means that even as a child his hair was white. For almost a century after his death his tomb was honoured, and he was England's favourite saint long before his canonisation in 1161. That was in the reign of Henry II, the Conqueror's great-grandson, who helped to carry the coffin on his shoulders to the high altar, where it was opened and the body found to be incorrupt, the pale hair and beard unchanged. A beautiful enamelled crucifix lay on the saint's breast, and they left it there. More than five hundred years later, in the reign of James II, Edward the Confessor's coffin was opened again. This time the king took the crucifix, and never returned it. Nobody knows where it is now.

However Edward the Confessor's tomb was one of the few spared by Henry VIII, who desecrated Becket's, a saint who with St. George, at the time of the Crusades, replaced Edward in the people's memory. He is perhaps more honoured today by visitors to the Abbey. He was last of the line of Cerdic and of Alfred the Great.

Edmund

St. Edmund is the name of two men, and the one who lived first is better remembered, although we know less about him than the second. This is because a famous abbey was built over his bones.

Edmund, king of East Anglia, was a German prince, son of a king named Alkmund. He was so handsome, and so good and wise, even as a boy, that he was adopted by Offa, king of Mercia (the one who built Offa's Dyke to keep out the wild Welsh). As had been the practice with the old Roman emperors, Offa made

Edmund his heir and successor. At that time there began to be trouble with pirate ships from Scandinavia, whose crews invaded England and pillaged towns and rich churches. Often they had a device of a raven on their sails, and to this day a raven is considered a sign of ill luck in East Anglia.

Edmund marched with an army against these pirates, and fought them at a place named Hoxne in Suffolk, in the year 870. They captured him after the battle and because he refused to deny Christ and become a pagan like themselves, they shot him to death with arrows. Another version says that he was a ritual victim to the pagan gods. Whichever happened, in 903 his remains were taken from Hoxne to St. Edmund's Bury, as it was called then, and a magnificent church, later an abbey, was erected over his remains. By then his cult had spread all over England, and all through the centuries gifts were brought to the abbey and many important persons were buried there, including a sister of Henry VIII. Later, when he ruined the abbey at the Reformation, Henry removed her coffin to a place outside. Today the place is known as Bury St. Edmunds, and it may interest you to know that a street in London where finance offices are, called Bevis Marks, is taken from a clerk's early mistake for Bury's Marks, in other words the boundary of land owned in London by St. Edmund's abbey.

The second of the name was St. Edmund Rich, who fell out with Henry III in much the same way as his predecessor Thomas Becket – they were both archbishops of Canterbury – had done with Henry II. However Edmund Rich was not as contentious a man as Becket, and instead of continuing to argue and hold out against the king, quietly retired to a French monastery, where he became much loved for the piety of his life, and unlike Becket was not murdered, but died in the same year as his retirement, 1240.

Francis

Ask any Frenchman about St. Francis and he may think first of St. Francis of Paola, who walked on water and performed other miracles in France at the time of Louis XI. Ask a Neapolitan, and he may well think of St. Francis Geronimo, the Jesuit who preached marvellously even on slave ships and was given a funeral in Naples grander than that of kings. In Goa and Japan they will remember St. Francis Xavier, the famous missionary. Writers will remember St. Francis de Sales, their patron.

Anyone in the world, however, will know the name of St. Francis of Assisi.

He lived earlier than either of the above, being born in 1182. His father was a merchant named Pietro Bernardone, and Pietro was successful enough in his business, which took him abroad, to have been permitted to marry a bride of grand connections in Picardy, then a district in France. She was always therefore known as Pica, though her real name was Jeanne or Giovanna. When their son was born his father was away on his travels with merchandise, so the child was christened Giovanni, or John, after his mother. However when Pietro returned he proudly caught his son up in his arms and said 'You are my little Francesco, my little Frenchman.' Francesco, or Francis, the boy remained.

His father gave him a good education, employing tutors to teach him French and Latin, also probably other languages to fit him for his expected future life as his father's assistant, travelling abroad with wares. In a way this was to come true, but not in the way Pietro expected. Meantime, the young Francesco became very well liked in his native town. He was a natural leader, had plenty of money and great charm. He was not tall – later he was to describe himself as 'the little poor man of Assisi' – but from the only portrait we know of which could have been painted by someone who knew him early in life, he was handsome except for having large ears. He had great compelling eyes, a persuasive mouth and slim neck. This hooded portrait, describing him only as *frater*, is to be seen on a wall fresco in the chapel of St. Gregory in Sacro Speco, Subiaco. Its date is the thirteenth century. A later portrait by Cimabue (1240-1302) who could not have known Francis in life but probably painted from a description of him, shows a man worn with hardship, travel, illness and penances, unrecognisable as the earlier version except for the noticeable ears.

Meantime, wars broke out constantly between Italian cities as they do between neighbouring countries today, generally over petty squabbles. One such broke out in 1202 between Assisi and its neighbour Perugia. Francis went with his friends to do battle with the Perugians, and ended up in prison, aged twenty. He spent at least a year in confinement and as many did, fell ill. In these conditions he began for the first time to think about himself, not in the former manner as a young man who might expect everything the world had to give, but why he was in the world at all. Nevertheless he did not yet give up his old life. In a later war with Apulia he started out again with the rest, but was recalled by a curious vision of a hall hung with armour. He turned back, and after that had other experiences; he met a leper, an outcast from humanity. Later on, Franciscans were to be noted for their bravery in nursing these, remaining unafraid of the dreaded infection. Francis about then also heard a voice from the cross at San Damiano, a church he was later to rebuild with many others.

By this time, he was beginning to become the person God intended. By 1206 he had fallen out with his father Pietro, who had grown hard and grasping and expected gratitude for all he had done for his son, a common failing. However he can hardly be blamed for thinking Francis a little odd when the latter, taunted about his ingratitude in leading his own life, offered to return even the clothes he had on. He cast them off in public and was hastily covered by a friend's cloak. Francis never lacked friends, and one accompanied him during the time he spent in reflection and prayer in caves and hidden crannies in the rocks. The friend is praised for having kept silent, which is often the best way of helping people. Nevertheless Francis soon knew that he was not to be a hermit in a cave, shut away from the world, but that God wanted him to go out into it, in a manner which had not been attempted since the time of the apostles. Francis was particularly influenced by the verses in Matthew 10, 5-14, when Christ tells his disciples to take no belongings with them at all on their first journey without him; to stay in the first house that makes them welcome, and if a town does not, to shake the dust from their feet.

This gave rise to Francis' conviction that he must take a vow of poverty. He had already seen the harm riches had done his father, and he came to hold the view that money was altogether evil. In practical fact, it cannot altogether be done without; Christ himself used it, as we know from at least two references in the Gospels apart from the one to the disciples to go and buy bread. One, too seldom read out in churches, is when he told Peter to go and catch a fish with a coin in its mouth in order to pay their temple tax, which was not really due (Matthew 17, 24-27), and the other, when Judas is said to have stolen money from the common purse (John 12, 6). Francis held such extreme views on the matter that when a desperate brother accepted some coins later on, Francis forced him to put them in his mouth and then go and spit them out on a dunghill. This seems going rather far; but what Francis really meant to teach was that it is wrong to attach more importance to the things of this world than to those of the next.

Having renounced anything he might expect from his angry and disappointed father, Francis attracted followers in exactly the way he had attracted friends in earlier days; as Christ had done it, by the charm of his personality. All who knew Francis of

Assisi loved him, no doubt even the abandoned Pietro. Much later on, a Pope was to describe Francis as *alter Christus*, the other Christ. The first form of his rule is no longer to be found, but by 1210 Pope Innocent III, a most zealous and forward-looking man, approved this very new idea indeed of an order which did not shut itself away in a monastery, but instead went about the streets and public ways preaching not only to the poor but to the rich, exactly as Christ had done while on earth.

This idea became so popular that Francis' followers swelled to great numbers, and as always happens in such cases tensions began to arise. The licence to preach, which the Pope had at first granted to all members of the new order of friars, was later to be confined to those who had studied at a university and had then undergone an approved examination (echoes arise of our present day). This was not what Francis had intended, and also, when he was elsewhere confusion arose among the rest, which shows how greatly needed he was personally. The Franciscan friars, with their tonsures and grey-brown habit, were by then a familiar sight in towns and countries well beyond Italy. Crowds thronged to listen, to do penance, to offer alms, money being forbidden. The alms usually took the form of food.

The heart of all this activity, the so-called cradle of the order, was at the Portiuncula, or Little Gate. A tremendous meeting, or chapter, was held at Mats, near Assisi, in 1221 to try, in other words, to sort everything out. More than 3,000 friars attended, among them an unknown Portuguese brother who strongly advised education for the friars in order that they might not be called ignorant for being poor. Later he was known as St. Anthony of Padua. Francis was eventually persuaded, and appointed Anthony professor of theology; he also began to appoint vicars-general, as his health was failing.

He had spared himself nothing and had gone on many travels. He was anxious to go to Syria; it was the time of crusades. The first journey ended in shipwreck and Francis was cast ashore in Dalmatia, a long way off. A second time, on the way to

Morocco, illness overtook him and he had to stay for a year in Spain, recovering. The third time – and by then the order had been expanded into provinces, was recognised as fully valid within a year or two, and he himself was famous throughout the known world – he reached Syria, got himself into the presence of the Sultan Malik-Al-Kamil, and preached to try to convert the latter to Christianity. He did not succeed, but won the Sultan's respect enough for his friars to be permitted to guard the Holy Sepulchre and, to a certain extent, to minister in Palestine. To this day it is full of Franciscans, whose part in the later crusades was heroic; they did not fight, but nursed the wounded, memorably the brave boy who was one of the last Christian kings to reign in Jerusalem. He was a leper, and won the last victory at Montgisard. When he slid from his horse exhausted, nobody dared touch him but the Franciscans who tended him. He died soon after, of his illness.

About Francis himself there are numberless stories, some we know to be true and others which may not be but which reflect the great love his followers, and other people, have for him. One shows that he must have been ordained, though we do not know when. He started the Christmas crib at Greccio on December 25th 1223, using a real ox and ass, real straw and a real baby. This shows his love for created things and the trust animals placed in him, a gift known as rapport. There is another story which may well be true; a fierce wolf had terrorised a neighbourhood for some time. Francis went to the wild place where it lived, talked to it in a friendly manner and persuaded it to follow him back to the town. 'Brother Wolf is hungry; give him something to eat,' he told them. Once fed, like any animal, the wolf gave no more trouble, and Francis made the town promise to keep it supplied with food. Everyone knows the story of his preaching to the birds; his poem, the Canticle of the Sun, shows his love for God's creation and the way the creation itself honours God. It is a sin against God to neglect or ill-treat an animal. In the earliest time of all, the whole of creation trusted;

the promise is that, again, the lion shall lie down with the lamb. No one was more aware of this than Francis, and in every Franciscan church in Palestine you are liable to be greeted by a dog wagging its tail by the door.

However other matters claimed the saint's attention. You may want to read in one of our other articles the story of St. Clare, the rich and beautiful young woman who founded the second order under the instruction of Francis. He himself did not live to be old. Worn out with his exertions and penances – he had issued constant circular letters of instruction after the manner of St. Paul, and like him journeyed unendingly – he began to become blind. Two years before his death, however, he was granted one most special vision. On a mountain named Alvernia (La Verna) on 14th September 1224, he received the stigmata during a vision of Christ. It is the earliest recorded evidence of this happening, which has only been granted to a very few.

Francis of Assisi died on 3rd October 1226. He was only forty-four. Next day he was buried in the church of San Giorgio, but later his remains were transferred to the lower church in Assisi. The site of the grave was kept secret lest robbers come for relics and as the centuries passed, its actual place became uncertain although devotion to Francis remained strong. The grave was not found, despite four separate official attempts, until as late as 1818.

The Feast of the Stigmata is on September 17th and that of Francis himself on 4th October, the day of his burial. There are other feast days connected with him including that of the finding of the grave. Francis had long before been canonised, less than two years after his death. He was declared *alter Christus* by Pope Pius XI in 1926. He is the patron saint of Catholic Action and, with St. Anthony, of animals. Besides Assisi, there is a famous shrine in Brazil where 40,000 pilgrims have been known to congregate in some years since miracles in the saint's name began there in 1795. All over the world there are missionaries inspired by 'the little poor man of Assisi'; and though they honour their vow of poverty, I have never met an unhappy Franciscan.

George

You will no doubt have heard of St. George as the patron saint of England. You will have seen his red-and-white flag, a cross which, together with that of St. Andrew, makes up the Union Jack. You may have seen his image slaying the dragon on the gold insignia of the Order of the Garter, which was founded by Edward III. That king, who died in 1377, also built the Round Tower at Windsor and dedicated it to St. George.

The odd thing is that this particular saint never existed, though several others of the name did.

The figure of a knight slaying a dragon, which is what you have probably seen — there may or may not be a princess in the background being rescued — was brought home from the East by the Crusaders as an ideal of chivalry. It is possible that the origin was the old Greek legend of Perseus, who rescued the king's daughter Andromeda from a dragon which was about to eat her. Also, in the East there is the legend of the young man called the Khidr, whose death brings a green harvest.

The Archangel Michael is traditionally shown slaying a dragon, and in a great many icons of St. George you will find him with wings. The story first appears in *The Golden Legend*, by a writer named Voragine.

For whatever reason, returning crusaders or not, the name of St. George became so closely associated with England (and with Portugal, where he has ousted the Apostle Thomas) that our former patron saint, St. Edward the Confessor, was almost forgotten. However St. Thomas of Canterbury, murdered about a hundred years afterwards, rivalled both Edward and George as a favourite saint not only in England, but all over Europe.

The real St. George may have been an early martyr tortured and killed in the persecutions of Diocletian, April 23rd 303. Otherwise he may have suffered at Lydda in Palestine, where his tomb is said to be. Gibbon, the historian of the later Roman Empire, confused St. George with an Arian bishop who was torn in pieces by angry crowds in Alexandria in 366.

One way and another, the name of George stood so certainly for England – 'St. George for merrie England' was a favourite saying of Charles II – that the Protestant heir to the throne was christened George by his mother, Sophia of Hanover. He became George I, and since then there have been five more kings of the name in Great Britain. Many of them have lived up to the ideal of chivalry which the crusaders brought home, and whatever its origin, the name of George is by now stoutly English.

Hugh

Henry II of England had been blamed, rightly or wrongly, for the murder of his Archbishop of Canterbury, Thomas Becket, in 1170. He was anxious to make amends to the Church, as they say, to improve his image. This was not easy, as he was close-fisted and moreover had a very bad temper. When he was really angry he used to tear off his clothes and chew the straw on the floor, as in those days there were no carpets. He was supposed to be descended from the devil.

However he invited some Carthusian brothers to come to England from Burgundy, where they lived in their mother house of the Grande Chartreuse. Their rule was strict, with fasting, prayer, reading, and manual labour. They remained silent except when in church or during their weekly walk. Otherwise they lived retired from the world.

It must have been a shock to the brothers to find, when they reached England, that the house the king had promised them, at Witham in Somerset, was being lived in by peasants who refused to move out. The poor monks built themselves what shelter they could among the woods and marshes, but the king sent them no money and although French was spoken then in England, it was not quite the same as in Burgundy. One way and another the monks' lives grew so hard that they thought of going back home.

At news of this, King Henry sent for the prior, a man named Hugh. Hugh was a person of deep humour and charm. Though nobody else, not even his own sons, could wring money out of Henry II, Hugh managed it. He also persuaded the peasants to move out, and recompensed them with some of the king's money so that they were able to find somewhere else to live. In these days of social security it is difficult to imagine what an unusual act this was. Peasants were considered as little more than animals, with few rights.

The new Carthusian friary prospered under Hugh, and when the king was passing that way he used to call in on the prior. One day, however, he heard that Hugh had excommunicated a forester, a royal official. There were good reasons, but the king flew into one of his rages, though he did not, that time, chew straw. He merely became so sullen that nobody dared address him. He rode off to the hunt, and Hugh followed alone. When he caught up with the courtiers, none of them would speak to him because they were afraid of the king.

Henry was sitting on the ground, stitching up a leather stall in which he had put a hurt finger. 'How like your cousins of Falaise you look!' remarked the prior.

Nobody else would have dared to say it. William the Conqueror, Henry's great-grandfather, had been descended from tanners in Falaise in Normandy, but it was of course never spoken of. However the king saw the funny side and rolled on the ground with laughter. In the end the forester was flogged, and continued great friends with Prior Hugh.

In the last year of his own life, Henry II made Hugh bishop of Lincoln, and, when he was canonised, it was as St. Hugh of Lincoln. Meantime the Carthusian Order flourished in England, and by the end nine houses were built. All of them suffered dreadfully at the hands of a later Henry, Henry VIII, in 1535. Carthusians are among the first English martyrs. At the London Charterhouse, at the last Mass at which they were left in peace, they heard the Holy Spirit pass like a whisper among them. It gave most of them strength to die for their faith after appalling treatment, though some fled abroad. One king named Henry brought them to England; another drove them out. It is doubtful whether even Prior Hugh could have saved the day by then.

James

There are two apostles of the name of James, the Great and the Less. This does not mean that one was more important than the other, only that one was short and one was tall! To take the least first, James the Less – 'little James', who became bishop of Jerusalem and was martyred about 62, was the son of Alphaeus or Cleopas (the names mean the same thing) and of Mary, the kinswoman of Our Lady. She was obviously not the latter's sister, as is sometimes wrongly stated; for one thing there would not be two girls named Mary in the same family, and for another the Immaculate Conception shows Our Lady as the only child of Joachim and Anne. Similar confusion used to arise when Jesus' 'brethren' were referred to. The word merely means a kinsman. Mary Cleopas, otherwise known as Mary Jacoby, mother of this James, is said to have journeyed to the south of France in a boat with three others after the Resurrection (see article on St. Sarah and the one on St. Mary Magdalene).

To turn to the taller James, he was the son of Zebedee and Mary Salomé, and the brother of John. The two brothers were fishermen, and left their nets to follow Christ at the same time as Andrew and Peter. Later on Jesus, in his witty way, called James and John Boanerges, the Sons of Thunder. This was because they had made a great deal of shouting about destroying a certain Samaritan town which refused to listen (Luke 9, 54). They were with Peter on the mountain at the Transfiguration, and afterwards at Gethsemane. On both occasions they were sleepy. Nevertheless James was the first of all to die for Christ, beheaded under Herod Agrippa in 44 A.D.

The story of his relics is even more important than the story of his life. It is recorded by a blind man named Didymus, which as in the case of Thomas means a twin, that James visited Spain in his lifetime after the Resurrection, but the visit must have been brief. It is probable that after his death, his remains were taken there, perhaps because he was remembered in that country and perhaps not. By the time Christian refugees were fleeing from the Arab invasions of the south in 711, they carried St. James's relics with them to Galicia, in the north. There is a legend that they were shipwrecked and that the relics were miraculously transported by sea, giving rise to the symbol of a cockleshell for future pilgrims to Compostela, where the relics were taken and a church built. It is probable that this first church was erected on a former pagan temple to Castor and Pollux, as recent excavations have revealed pre-Christian remains. This church, except for St. James's tomb, was destroyed in 997, but there had been pilgrimages to the site for almost fifty years. They continued over the centuries, and many of the pilgrims were saints and kings. The Empress Maud, widow of Emperor Henry the Lion, later to fight for her rights as heiress of England, came, and took away a hand of the saint she later presented to her father, Henry I, at Winchester. Louis VII of France came; before that, so had Ss

Dominic and Francis in their time. The routes to Compostela can still be followed and many of the old hospices remain; from Paris by way of Orléans, Tours, Poitiers, Bordeaux, Roncesvalles – where 30,000 meals a year for pilgrims were provided – Pamplona, Burgos, Léon, and at last Compostela. Other pilgrimages, with a cockleshell fastened in one's hat, began from Vézelay where the crusades were preached; Le Puy and Arles by way of Toulouse. On arrival, the grandest of all hospices awaited those who had come so far; the Gran Ospidale Real, built by Ferdinand and Isabella in the fifteenth century. It is still there, and echoes the grandeur of the cathedral across one side of the great square, begun in 1075 over the tomb, and completed in 1211. Today, after the 12 o'clock Mass there, they have the joyful ceremony of the Botafumeiro, with eight vergers pulling hard on side ropes to raise a strong middle one, from which hangs an immense shining censer the size of a man. It ascends to the roof like a great bell, while the organ, some of whose pipes lie flat like those of a spinet, peals out music. Incense is scattered through the round upper arches, the vaulting, the space of the great nave. St. James – Santiago de Compostela, his name in Spanish, former battle-cry against the Moors – waits above the high altar, silver-hooded and carrying his sword. Below, down a flight of steps, in a tiny chapel to be visited privately, are his relics, verified by Pope Leo XIII in 1884. There is an exultant sense of the joy of God, less perhaps because of their presence than because so many, all through the centuries, have journeyed here with devotion and prayer. It is a long way from the fishermen's nets of Galilee.

John

'In the beginning was the Word, and the Word was with God, and the Word was God.'

The opening of St. John's Gospel shows his perfect understanding of the Trinity. It is different from the others, which deal mainly with facts. This understanding, which also brought him to the foot of the Cross when the rest had fled, may well be the reason why he, the Beloved Disciple, was given the charge of Our Lady at the Crucifixion.

However Jesus' words 'What is it to you if he tarry till I come?' made earlier, were, like many of his sayings, taken with solemn literalness by the other disciples. They took them as a proof that John was to live forever. The tale may be compared with that of the Wandering Jew, said to have been met with by inmates of Nazi prison camps in the Second World War.

John probably went to Ephesus with Our Lady, and after the Assumption may have visited the island of Patmos, where there is a monastery now. However if you go there, you will find that the people of this small island maintain that the Book of Revelation was written not by the Apostle John, but by a visionary known as John the Divine, who lived there in the sixth century and whose portrait hangs in the cave where the visions were seen.

There have been many Johns in Christian history, some of them its greatest saints. There was St. John Nepomuk, drowned for refusing to reveal the secrets of the confessional; St. John Ogilvie, hanged in 1615; St. John of God, St. John of the Cross, friend and counsellor to St. Teresa. Nevertheless the first of them all, though Christ said he would be the last in the kingdom of heaven, is St. John the Baptist, the Forerunner.

Like many children of promise in the Bible, he was born to an elderly woman till then thought barren. Our Lady, after the Annunciation, journeyed to be with her cousin Elizabeth at the birth of the latter's child. The place of the Visitation is now thought to have been up a steep hill. When the unborn Christ approached, the unborn John leaped in the womb. Some say that because of this, he was born without original sin. There is a cave still shown today where St. Elizabeth is said to have hidden with him during the Massacre of the Innocents under Herod.

As you know, the Baptist grew up into a solitary, wearing a rough covering of camel's hair and living in the desert on locusts and wild honey. (This was not a bad diet; fried locusts are still a delicacy in the Middle East.) However John preached the need for repentance and baptism. By many he was thought to be the prophet Elijah (Elias) come again. The place in the Jordan where he baptised Christ, the Lamb of God, is the same today; a deep pool fringed by willows. In those times the baptised person was immersed totally.

John spoke humbly of his own unworthiness to untie Christ's sandals, but was fiercely outspoken to others when needed, no matter who they were. His words angered Herod, who had him arrested and, later, beheaded. Oscar Wilde has written a play about this, and an old film by Pasolini, *The Gospel According to Matthew*, shows Salomé as a young girl dancing with a bough of cherry blossom in her hand, beguiling the jaded king. Jesus grieved greatly at his cousin's death.

Many famous paintings have been made of the Holy Family, often including John the Baptist. Although Jesus said that he would be the last in heaven, he only meant that others can get there as well.

John Ogilvie

St. John Ogilvie was born in the north of Scotland in about 1578. His father was Sir Walter Ogilvie of Drum-na-Keith in Banff. His mother had been Agnes Elphinstone, a devout Catholic in days when life was difficult and dangerous for these. She died in childbirth when her son was too small to remember her, but he and his baby sister were brought up by their aunt, who was also a Catholic and taught the children their prayers and the rosary, telling them also about the forbidden Mass which could only be heard now and again in secret when a priest dared to land in Scotland from abroad. If he was caught, he was under sentence of death, and in England this was carried out. Meantime in Scotland they were usually imprisoned for a time and then set free on condition that they did not return.

When John Ogilvie was about eight years old his father married again. His bride was one of the Seven Pearls of Lochleven, beautiful sisters who lived in the island castle from which Mary, Queen of Scots, had twice made her escape, only to end by being imprisoned for life in England and, later, executed. John would hear whispers of the execution about the time of his father's new marriage. No doubt his stepmother had harsh things to say about the Catholic queen, as she herself had been reared as a Calvinist. Meantime Queen Mary's son James, from whom she had been separated as a baby so that he never knew her, was made king of Scots and later, at the death of Elizabeth, king of England as James I. He was a strange man, very learned, but his boyhood had been cruel and he was concerned, more than anything else, for his own safety. Later John Ogilvie was to come to know him as well as anyone could.

The Pearl of Lochleven had meantime made several changes in John's life. Firstly she had borne his father a son, James, whom she wanted to inherit John's title and estate. Meantime her husband Sir Walter, no doubt because of his Calvinist marriage, was made one of the King's officials 'to harry the Papists, and in particular the Jesuits' found in that part of the north. It was therefore awkward for Sir Walter that his eldest son should be one of the first-named. He listened to the advice of his wife and decided that John should be sent abroad to his uncle, his mother's brother, who had been Superior at Douai and was by then Rector of the Scots College at Rome. John, who was twelve years old, was not told that he was never to be allowed to return home.

He was put on board ship at an east-coast port, carrying a letter to his uncle the Rector and with some money given him by his father to keep him till he should have reached Rome. Unluckily the letter, however it was sent, never reached George Elphinstone. John's money was soon finished, he was alone in a strange land, and no further word came from his father at home. In fact, by then, all evidence of John's existence had been destroyed and it was his young half-brother James who was made the heir. John Ogilvie would only be remembered by his young sister Christian, who was married off shortly to a Calvinist laird. A few would also remember seeing the bright-haired boy riding or walking about the near hills. No one who had met him ever forgot the intensely blue colour of his eyes, their kindly glance, or his laughter. He had a deep sense of humour which was to stand him in good stead in the times that followed.

Meantime, he was starving. It is possible that he tried to walk to Rome. One night he huddled, wrapped in his cloak, on the doorstep of a house in Helmütz, a town between Germany and France. He knew no German, and when the woman of the house came out to chase him away, could not get her to understand that all he needed was a crust of bread and, if possible, shelter.

John Ogilvie

She pointed up the street to where there was a monastery John had not known of. He made his way there and heard, inside, the sound of chanting. By then it was almost dawn.

The monks let him in and gave him a pallet on which to sleep, also some food if he would help to sweep and clean. He did this and, fortunately, one of the brothers spoke a little Scots. This brother took John to the abbot, whom between them they persuaded to write a letter to Rector George Elphinstone in Rome. This time it arrived, and uncle and nephew met at last. Meantime, in the monastery, John had been made aware of what it was God wanted him to do. He must become a priest, and return to Scotland as a missionary. He knew even then what it would mean in the end, but from that time on nothing made him change his mind.

First of all it would be necessary to study abroad, and he applied to the college at Louvain. They accepted him, but soon it became clear that they had run out of funds and could not continue. After a year, John had to find somewhere else. Finally he joined the Benedictine community at Ratisbon, but they also were going through hard times. Although John enjoyed the scholarship he found there and could already speak and write Latin from his own early education in Scotland, he knew that the cloistered life was not for him. He needed to be out in the world, ministering to ordinary folk.

At some time he learned about Ignatius Loyola, the wounded soldier who had practised severe austerities on himself in a cave and had then gone back to school with children to learn Latin. Ignatius had thereafter founded the Society of Jesus, soldiers of God. John resolved to join them if they would accept him, perhaps remembering his father's enmity. The training was long, but would develop his fine mind to deal with any situation and would discipline his body to endure it. Total obedience to his superiors would be demanded, and in this John was afterwards thought somewhat to fail; he was determined to go back to Scotland, but the Society had other ideas for him. Nevertheless he was inspired by the example of Edmund Campion, S.J., who had been betrayed, tortured and finally martyred in England; also Father Henry Garnet, hanged there for refusing to reveal the confessions of one of the so-called Gunpowder Plotters, trapped as they had been by King James's minister Cecil with the intention of forcing the king to be harder on Catholics than he was. James, terrified at the thought of gunpowder, which had earlier been involved in the murder of his father Darnley, thereafter allowed Cecil to do as he would. Nevertheless in Scotland there were as yet no martyred Catholic priests. John himself was to be the first and, so far, the last of them.

Meantime, his reception into the Society was not easy. After study for some years in Moravia – its equivalent is roughly Czechoslovakia today – plague broke out in the city of Olmütz, where John Ogilvie and his fellow-students were. The Superior, fearful of catching the plague, had himself carried immediately by litter to Vienna, a long way off. John Ogilvie determinedly followed him on horseback. By now he was a handsome young man, bearded and with reddish hair and broad shoulders. The journey involved difficult mountain passes, mud and stony paths and marshes, but John travelled on. When at last he saw the spires of Vienna he and his horse were exhausted, but he was triumphant. His Superior was astonished, and perhaps ashamed, when the young Scot knelt before him. He allowed him to take the vows of poverty, chastity and obedience and to enter the Society of Jesus at once.

Later, the new Jesuit – he had by then been one for five years – was at last allowed, though his superiors were unwilling, to return to Scotland. He landed at Leith, disguised as a horse-dealer named Watson (he later became very fond of using Watson). He did not attempt to revisit his old home of Drum. He went instead to his kinsman Patrick Grant of Ballindalloch, near Elgin, and then to the Earl of Huntly's seat of Strathbogie. At both of these places he said Mass, the latter at Christmas; folk came down from all directions across the hills, and John heard confessions which could not have been made for years. He then rode south.

This was not a part of his instruction, and he was later reproached for it in Paris by his Superior, Father Huntly, a kinsman of the Earl. Nevertheless Cecil, the King's minister and great enemy of Catholics, was newly dead, and John Ogilvie hoped that if he himself could gain an audience with the king, he might persuade James to be less hard on Catholics in England and in Scotland. He obtained entry to court and, what was more difficult, an audience with King James himself. The latter gave him a pass to go overseas and to return.

John went to Paris, to tell Father Huntly that the king had made certain promises; but he was received coldly and instructed to return to Scotland, where he had been so anxious to go. He was nothing loth, and having failed with Father Huntly used the king's pass to return.

Thereafter he undertook the care of souls in Glasgow and Edinburgh. In the capital he lodged in a house in the Canongate and disguised himself as tutor to his host's two boys. The time allowed him was short. It was in Glasgow that he was betrayed by a man who had joined in his secret Masses.

His experiences after that were those of Christ. On first being taken he was spat upon and his beard pulled. Later he was chained in prison by the ankles and deprived of sleep: this was done by sticking pins under his fingernails and, when even that failed, dragging him back and forth on the floor. This went on for nine days and nights. The object was to deprive him of his sharp wits, but this they did not manage, although at one point the torture known as The Boot was applied; it was said to make the marrow of the bone spurt out of the leg, and at his trial one of Ogilvie's legs was seen to be swollen. In prison, someone drew the only portrait of him that is certainly known, but owing to the lack of sleep the eyes are rolled up in his head, his face is drawn and narrow, and his hair and beard have been shaved because of the lice in prison. Many do not realise that this is not his ordinary appearance. They also stole his cloak, and made him appear in a short torn one instead.

Despite all this, the answers he gave at the trial were so spirited and apt that they confounded the judges; a full account can be read as written by Father Ogilvie himself, secretly in prison and in chains. He used to thrust the written pages under the door at a worn place on the step, trusting that they would be found and taken by a friend, which they were. These notes prove that John Ogilvie was not hanged for treason, as his enemies tried to make out, but for his religion. He was also able to make this clear on the scaffold, though he had been forbidden to speak.

He was hanged at Glasgow Tolbooth on 28th February 1615. It is supposed that it was King James's influence that prevented the customary drawing and quartering. Ogilvie faced death bravely, having been given absolution by an agreed signal from a fellow-priest in the crowd. He climbed the high ladder with his hands tied behind his back, reciting prayers in Latin and then translating them so that the crowds below could understand. The streets were packed, and before being turned off the ladder John Ogilvie threw his rosary into the crowd. It struck a young Hungarian, who was a Calvinist but who later became a Catholic, saying he could never forget John Ogilvie or his death. Shortly before it, Ogilvie had said 'I hope to come back to Glasgow and to do more good there.' This speech puzzled his hearers; how could a man who was about to be hanged come back?

Nevertheless he has done so. Among other miracles, in 1965 a man named John Fagan was dying of cancer of the stomach. His wife pinned a medal of Blessed John Ogilvie, as he had been since 1929, to Fagan's pyjamas, and prayed. Shortly Fagan was pronounced cured; the details are in the press of the time. It took a further delay of almost twenty years for St. John Ogilvie to be proclaimed in the Vatican. At the canonisation, with St. Peter's packed with Scots, two pipers piped in the Pope to the tune of

Scotland the Brave, and one of them burst into tears! This great occasion was, by now, a further twenty years ago. Last year, the writer experienced a personal cure after praying to Our Lady and St. John Ogilvie.

If you want to read more, ask at the library for THE MAN FROM THE NORTH, a novel which tells this story in more detail. Meantime, you have chosen a good name; live up to it. The March Walk in Glasgow takes place every year, on the anniversary of the martyrdom as altered by the new calendar.

Joseph

It is said of some people that if they had not existed, it would be necessary to invent them. That nobody invented St. Joseph, that he lived and was the husband of Mary, can be seen from his pedigree, which is set out in such detail in the Gospel of Matthew that Joseph's descent from King David, and indeed from Adam, is clear.

As a Son of David, a member of David's line, he had a particular standing that had nothing to do with poverty or riches. Just as the tribe of Levi were priests by inheritance, so the line of the unforgotten David was unlike any other. David, despite his faults, had been beloved of God, had been preferred to Saul, had been a shepherd and a king, the sweet psalmist of Israel. His descendants were to fulfil the promises made much earlier to Abraham, who had not been perfect either, and foretold in the later prophecies, particularly those of Isaiah. There would be a Messiah born of David's line, who would redeem Israel. At the time, that was all anyone understood.

That Joseph was trained to a trade did not mean that he was uneducated, or a stupid person. Every educated Jew learned a trade. St. Paul was a tentmaker. St. Joseph was a carpenter, no doubt also a bricklayer. Upper-class English families of the last few centuries would have nothing to do with trade. The Jews were different; as Jesus himself said, the workman is worthy of his hire. Joseph, in other words, was what we now call a gentleman. This can be seen from what we know of him. He was also a hard worker.

Probably by reason of his steady character and reputation, he was chosen to be the guardian, or betrothed, of a young girl who, as she was a late-born only child, had been dedicated to Temple service, as had happened long before with Samuel. Her father Joachim had died and she had no protector. The story of the staff that burst into flower for the choice of Joseph may not be myth; the same thing had happened with Aaron's rod, which was still kept in the Holy of Holies.

It has been argued that because Jesus was not the son of Joseph but the Son of God, he was not a Son of David. It is not a point that matters very much except for people who like to split hairs, but in fact Mary was probably related to Joseph and of the same tribe. Both of them belonged to the Anawim, that portion of the Jewish people which had never worshipped the false gods of the king of Babylon during the captivity. The term in Hebrew came to mean 'poorest of the poor'. Mary herself is known to have supplied many details to St. Matthew for the writing of his account, and the accurate knowledge of the descent from David means that she knew it by heart and it was also probably her own.

We know what happened after the betrothal; how Joseph was perturbed to find that his betrothed was pregnant, as it was the last thing he would have expected of her; and of how he was told in a dream not to worry. The fact that he heeded the angel's advice shows us a good deal about him; he was humble enough to believe what he did not fully understand. Thereafter he knew that his duty was to guard Mary from all danger, including much to be met on the long journey to Bethlehem, where he had been born, to register for the emperor's tax. Lacking any comfortable place for the birth when they got there was probably the last straw, or would have been for an impatient man. Joseph merely kept his ears open and heard of a cave.

He is never absent from paintings of the stable, the shepherds and the kings. He is always shown as an older man. Once again instructed in a dream, 'he took the young child and his mother, and departed into Egypt.' While they stayed there, out of the way of Herod, Joseph probably plied his trade among the Egyptians, returning with his wife and the child only when it was safe. It was probably a little boy who had just learnt to walk, not an infant, who was presented in the Temple and who was seen by Simeon and Anna as the light of the Gentiles and the glory of Israel. The presentation of a tiny baby would have meant a dangerous double journey in great haste.

They returned to Nazareth. It was not what is known as an up-market area. Possibly Joseph decided to go there because the child would be safer in the north parts, but not Bethlehem where he might be recognised by relations. By then Herod was dead, and the quiet and busy Hidden Years followed, with Joseph working at his trade to support the family and teaching it to Jesus when the boy was old enough. It was probably he who saw to it that Jesus was well educated, with the prodigious learning of a Pharisee.

The relationship between Mary and Joseph is sensitively and beautifully expressed in a novel by Norah Lofts, HOW FAR TO BETHLEHEM? Try to get it from the library; it was written about 25 years ago. Again, the splitters of hairs, or dancers on the head of a pin, try to say that Mary had other children by Joseph. They lose sight of the fact that the word 'brother' (or sister) is the same as 'kinsman' in Aramaic. Mary the mother of James was Our Lady's kinswoman, not her sister; there would not have been two girls named Mary in the same family. Likewise James was not the 'brother' of Our Lord in any sense but that of a kinship in the family. If indeed Mary had had other children, why did Jesus, at the Crucifixion, give her into the care of John?

That was still far off at the time we hear the last of St. Joseph;

when he returned with Mary to search for the lost boy in Jerusalem, and found him sitting among the Temple doctors. Both of them, in course of the troubled search, must have recalled the words of the holy woman Anna to Our Lady; *And a sword shall pierce thy heart also*. But that time was not yet.

St. Joseph had almost certainly died by the commencement of Jesus' ministry. We do not know a single word that this quiet man said. At the apparitions at Knock in Ireland, he was shown standing to the left, and a little behind, Our Lady and St. John, the last wearing a low mitre such as was used in early times. St. Joseph is represented as an old man, with thick white hair, a short beard, and an air of humble dignity. As a friend once said to me 'Imagine being the only person in the house with original sin!'

St. Joseph is the patron of workers. This might be expected, but there was a reason in addition. His feast day is May-day, and to show their contempt for the Church this date was chosen by the communists as Labour Day. Pope Pius XII, who was always alert to the needs of the time, countered by setting May 1st aside as the Feast of St. Joseph the Worker, in 1955.

He would be honoured by us in any case.

Justin

Justin Martyr was one of the very early fathers of the Church. His death took place in Rome in 165. His father had been a Greek named Priscus, so from a boy Justin was familiar with Greek thought, especially that of Plato.

While walking one day on the seashore, Justin met an old man who spoke to him at length about the Old Testament prophets. As he was already impressed by the heroic sufferings of the

Christian martyrs, Justin became a Christian himself. He went on to teach Christian philosophy, one of the first to do so, in Ephesus till after 135. There must still have been people living in that pleasant town, whose sloping streets were washed daily, who remembered their fathers or grandfathers speaking of having known St. John and Our Lady when they lived there after the Crucifixion. Justin accepted the Virgin Birth as part of his belief.

Later on he went to Rome, and taught from his house on the Viminal. There he had a famous argument with a Cynic philosopher named Crescens. The Cynics – there are still some today – did not believe that anything could be pleasant. They scorned comfort, morality, the arts, and life itself. One of the most famous of them, Diogenes, you may have heard of; he finished by living in a tub.

Justin was well able to confound these dreary people, but about then he was betrayed to the city prefect, Rusticus. He had perhaps asked for trouble by sending written arguments to two of the emperors, Marcus Aurelius and Hadrian. The manuscript to the latter still survives. Both emperors were interested in philosophy, but neither were prepared to allow Christianity, as it denied that the emperor was divine.

Justin was martyred, therefore; but his ideas live after him. It must be remembered that he was one of the very first Christian thinkers, and some of his thoughts were later corrected by St. Augustine as they had given rise to a heresy called Arianism. It does not follow, however, that Justin was totally wrong.

He states that Christianity fulfils the highest hopes of Plato, who he believes learned from Moses the mystery of the Trinity. Christ is the divine Logos, the 'other God' mentioned in the Old Testament. The nature of God does not change and is beyond time and space. God created the world, and the soul has free will. Ignorant persons have the gift of supernatural revelation, but the seeds of truth are to be found in everyone endowed with reason (even the Cynics!). Gifted persons receive more truth.

Justin claims that Socrates and Abraham were Christians before Christ. He can see a divine plan in history. Old Testament and Greek thought combined make Christianity, he claims.

Nevertheless he mentions the Sacrament of Christ's flesh and blood, taken to absent members, and the kiss of peace. The mixing of water with the wine he says is because Christians were accused of drunkenness. We are taught now that the water represents humanity.

The cult of Mithras was prevalent in the time of Hadrian, and Justin calls the Mithraic bread and water a 'diabolical counterfeit.' No doubt this got him into trouble with the authorities; he never minced words. His feast day is on April 14th, and if you have chosen his name you are helping to ensure that he is not forgotten.

Later Byzantine emperors, after the time of Constantine, used the name Justin themselves.

Luke

In the Middle Ages, kings and knights used to choose their own special oath and always used it. The one chosen by William the Conqueror was 'by the splendour of God'. His son William Rufus, said to be one of our wickedest kings – he was probably a pagan and like King John, refused to take the Sacrament at his coronation – may have been unwilling to use the name of God. He used to swear instead *per vultum Lucano*, by the face of Luke. This, whether the Red King knew it or not, meant not St. Luke's face but Christ's. It is said that Nicodemus pressed a linen cloth over the dead face of Jesus after his body was taken down from the Cross. The cloth later passed into the possession of St. Luke. The story is of course a variant on that of St. Veronica (see our article).

Luke

Luke was a man of many parts; artist, physician and writer. His Gospel is said to be the most brilliantly expressed of all four. Although he probably never set eyes on Jesus himself, he almost certainly obtained much of his narrative straight from Our Lady; there are things mentioned in it which no one else could have known. There is the visit of the angel Gabriel, who later visited her also, to the Baptist's father Zachary, striking him dumb; there is the exact timing of the Visitation to St. Elizabeth; the story of the birth at Bethlehem, no room at the inn; the adoration of the shepherds, and again the presence of angels; the later meeting with Simeon and Anna in the Temple, and the saying, which by then had come true, 'a sword shall pierce they heart also'. The story of Christ as a boy in the Temple, disputing with the doctors, is told, and the later one at Nazareth with his saying 'Physican, heal thyself'. We can imagine the talks between Mary and Luke, the memories that came from her which she had kept in her heart.

Luke's Gospel, said to be one of the earliest, is however placed third in the Testament series. Luke was probably also the writer of part of the Book of Acts. He was certainly the companion of St. Paul, and the description of the Last Supper in Luke 22.19 and Corinthians I, 11.23 is almost identical. Ernest Renan, a later biographer of Christ in the nineteenth century, calls St. Luke's 'the most literary of the Gospels'. However Renan's own book shocked many people when it came out.

The tradition that Luke was an artist may be the truth, whether or not work attributed to him is his. A head of Christ in the catacombs, a profile little known, is said to be by him. The round shape of the skull greatly resembles that produced in 3D by scientific photography in our own century on the Shroud. The features are similar to those we know. St. Luke could have heard an exact description of her son from Christ's mother, apart from the legend of the linen cloth. A very old portrait of Our Lady herself, kept in Santa Maria Maggiore in Rome, is said also to have been by St. Luke, although this is doubted by the people who always raise doubts.

St. Luke's symbol is that of the humble ox, which after all was a beast for all seasons.

Mark

The symbol of St. Mark is a lion. His Gospel is placed second in the New Testament, and it is believed that he was for a time St. Peter's secretary after the events following the Crucifixion, and wrote down many of the latter's memories of Jesus. Peter refers to him in his own Epistle as 'Mark my son' which meant that he was very fond of him.

We know in fact that Mark was the cousin of Barnabas, that his mother was called Mary and that she had a house in Jerusalem which was often used by the apostles (Acts 12.12 ff). However Mark had perhaps followed Jesus secretly, as he is not mentioned by name earlier. It is possible that he was the young man who escaped at Jesus' arrest and fled naked, leaving behind him the linen cloth he wore. Certainly someone other than the sleeping disciples must have witnessed the Agony in the Garden, and Mark's Gospel describes it at first hand.

The bulk of his Gospel is often humorous, showing Jesus' own sense of humour. It was read aloud for this reason some time ago in a series on Radio 3.

When the apostles began their missionary journeys, Mark accompanied his cousin Barnabas and the new man, Paul, as far as Pergas in Pamphylia. However everyone did not get on with Paul – St. Peter and he fell out remarkably later on – and Mark left them at Perga in Pamphylia, and returned home. On a second journey Paul declined his company, and the two cousins went alone to Cyprus, where they converted the governor himself, Sergius Paulius. One wonders if they encountered Lazarus, who is supposed to have gone to that island and to be buried there, having never been seen to smile again after having looked on death already. By then, Jerusalem had been destroyed as Christ had prophesied, and Mark is next heard of in Rome, at last in close company with Paul, whose heroic journeyings, writings, preaching and sufferings had at last removed the suspicion with which he had at first been regarded by some of the original followers of Jesus. We know that Paul was executed in Rome, but the fate of Mark is uncertain. He is however remembered in his great cathedral in Venice, where the lions, taken from Constantinople by the crusaders, look out over the piazza.

Martin

St. Martin of Tours was born about 316 in what is now Hungary. Then it was a Roman province, Pannonia. Martin's father was an army tribune, which meant that his son's future was expected to be in the army. Martin was fortunate in that, although his family were not Christian, he grew up in a new age of Christian toleration; the Edict of Constantine came about when he was a small boy.

He was educated at Pavia – officers and their families moved long distances, as had happened to Constantine himself – and when he became an army recruit, received promotion early both as the son of an officer, and because he performed his duties well. He was considerate of his men, and one bitterly cold day went round on inspection of the stables for them, wearing his warm scarlet officer's cloak. Huddled against the wall he saw a beggar.

We will never know what prompted the act which was to change Martin's life. He dismounted, cut his cloak in half with his sword and gave half to the beggar. We can imagine that he was in trouble with the commander, Julian, for damaging army property. That night Martin had a vision of Christ wearing the split cloak. 'What ye do unto one of the least of these, ye do unto me.'

Thereafter Martin asked for permission to resign from the army. He was accused of cowardice, because a campaign was about to be renewed against the Alemanni, who had been formerly overcome by the emperor's father. However in the end, Martin was free to study under Hilary of Poitiers, the great enemy of Arianism.

This was one of the less pleasant heresies, and it is noteworthy that it sprang up just as Christianity was freed. Its founder, Arius, had been a joyless creature described as 'tall, gloomy, fanatical, with downcast eyes and tangled hair' who sang his beliefs in a kind of chant. Some of them survive today, and the Emperor Constantine took the heresy so seriously that he called the Council of Nicaea to decide whether its beliefs were right or wrong, especially as his sister encouraged them. The Council decided that they were wrong, and set out the Nicene Creed. The battle continued, but Arius died in the midst of the argument. His companion, Eusebius, fled to Gaul, where he continued to preach the heresy. It spread so far that Martin himself was troubled by it when he returned to Pannonia, his native country. Like Christ when he went back to Nazareth, he was not made welcome.

He went to Italy, then Gaul. In 360 he founded a monastery near Poitiers. All this time his fame was spreading, and he is known to have worked many miracles. By the time he had been in his monastery eleven years, he was forced to leave it and to become bishop of Tours, a much larger place. Here he continued his miracles, and, again like Christ, got away from the crowds when he could. At last he found a cave near Marmoutiers, where he could be left in peace.

It is important to know that St. Ninian, the great apostle of south-west Scotland, visited him near the end of his life. Although he had considerable trouble from the Arian, Eusebius, in Gaul, the holiness of Martin's life made him much beloved. When he died, his monks put the body on a raft to float it down the river to Tours, and it is said that the flowers on the banks bowed down as it passed and that music was heard in the sky. By then, it was the year 400.

It is not generally known that St. Martin is responsible for the word chapel, *capella*. St. Louis, in the 13th century, took the split half of the famous cloak to Paris and built the Sainte Chapelle to house it and other relics such as the headband of plaited rushes which had tied the crown of thorns – it was more of a cap, probably bashed into shape over a Roman helmet and then put roughly on – to Christ's head. The Sainte Chapelle, the Holy Chapel, is still there in Paris, but the relics have gone. They were destroyed in the French Revolution of 1793. However the word itself is a reminder of the young Roman soldier who gave half his cloak to a beggar on a cold winter's day.

Matthew

St. Matthew's Gospel is placed first among the four, for the good reason that he set down more of Christ's actual sayings than any of the rest. This was due to the fact that he had the precise mind that remembers details, the mind of a tax-collector.

He belonged to this profession not by chance, but by inheritance. He was of the tribe of Levi. This tribe were by tradition priests according to the law of Moses, and therefore entitled to exact tithes. These are still exacted today from landowners, who pay them in England to the Church of England

and in Scotland to the Church of Scotland. This happens whether they belong to the churches or not, and so a lot of ill feeling is aroused. In Christ's time, there was ill feeling also, as there often is about money. Not all the tax-gatherers were honest; some kept money they were not entitled to, also kept it from widows and other people too poor to be able to help themselves in the matter. Christ's speech to the Pharisees makes this point clear. However it does not follow that Matthew himself was a dishonest tax-collector, though he seems to have been fairly well off.

We read that just after Jesus had cured the paralytic let down by his friends through a roof to avoid the crowds, who had been told 'Take up your bed and walk', Jesus came past the custom house, where Matthew was seated at his collecting-table. He said, as he had said to the fishermen 'Follow me,' and Matthew rose, left his piled money, and followed. Luke goes on to say that he then gave a large party for Jesus at his house. It was the natural instinct of a hospitable Jew; and it must have been, as they say, some party. I once went to a Jewish wedding where there were fourteen courses for dinner. On this occasion Matthew had invited his fellow Levites, other Pharisees and lawyers. This shows that he had courage, as already there was murmuring among the Pharisees about this Nazarene who said he could forgive sins and whose followers broke the Sabbath. Even Nicodemus, one of their number, only dared visit Jesus by night; but Matthew gave a party and asked everybody. Some of the guests were ungrateful enough to complain that Jesus kept company with tax-gatherers! There were also sinners, like Mary Magdalene, and others who had forsaken their former ways to follow Jesus. His swift reply was typical; it was not the healthy who needed a doctor, he told them, but the sick.

Matthew was one of those who remained with Jesus when many forsook him; he may have felt, as Peter put it 'Lord, to whom else shall we go? You have the words of eternal life.' He remained among the Twelve, although despite his knowledge of money it was not he who was put in charge of the common purse, but Judas, who stole from it, as John tells us. Perhaps Matthew wanted nothing more to do with money; he must have seen the rich young man who turned away because he had great possessions.

Matthew is not mentioned at the Crucifixion or the events that led up to it, and we do not know whether or not he was one of the two men on the road to Emmaus. Later on he preached what he remembered of Christ's sayings, and is said to have dictated them to a Greek secretary who translated them into that tongue. Also, he is thought to have contributed part of the Book of Hebrews; it is even possible to try to make out which might be his sayings and which St. Paul's. 'Today if ye hear his voice, harden not your hearts' could be an echo of the time, long before, when Matthew sat at his counting-table; there are many references to his tribe of Levi; and, most of all, it is mentioned there that Christ was sacrificed outside the city gate, like the former offerings of goats and bulls. Matthew must have seen this, with the rest, from a distance. St. Paul was not there.

We do not know how Matthew died, but he preached to the Hebrews and probably fell victim to their anger in the end, like his master. His symbol is the head of a man, Mark's a lion, Luke's an ox, and John's an eagle, sometimes carrying a fish in its claws. It is interesting to remember that the first and last Gospel writers knew one another best.

Michael

Michael is the chief of the seven archangels, the recorder. The belief in him is very old. The season of Michaelmas used to be held on September 29th, but the new calendar has changed it to

October 11th. You all know the Michaelmas daisy, which flowers later than the rest.

It is impossible not to believe in angels if one has faith, as they are not only beings without a physical presence who are at the bidding of God, but often through history, and in our personal experience, can act as messengers or protectors; do not forget your guardian angel. The Feast of St. Michael and All Angels shows, again, that Michael is their leader. He is mentioned several times in the Old Testament, being known as the guardian prince of Israel (Daniel 10, 21) and in the same prophet 12, 1 'at that time shall he stand up, the great prince who standeth for the children of the people'.

He has left several signs for us nearer England. He seems to have stood on eminences or flown over them. There is St. Michael's Mount in Cornwall, and opposite, across the Channel, Mont St. Michel on the borders of Brittany. The great archangel flew over both, and is also said to have stood on Mount Gedron during a battle of the Israelites, the race under his protection. His tasks seem to be different from those of Raphael, who guided Tobias in the Old Testament tale, or Gabriel, who appeared not only to Our Lady at the Annunciation, but before that to Zachary, father of John the Baptist; and who is said to be the one to sound the Last Trump at the final judgment.

To quote the Letter of Jude, who knew Christ, in verse 9 'In contrast, when the archangel Michael was in debate with the devil disputing the possession of Moses' body, he did not presume to condemn him in insulting words, but said 'May the Lord rebuke you!' This may be one of the things the disciples learned from Jesus, who said he had watched, long before his time on earth, Satan fall like lightning from the sky. This was at the time of the rebellion of certain angels against God.

In the Book of Revelation, 12, 7, it says 'Then war broke out in heaven. Michael and his angels made war upon the dragon. The dragon and his angels fought, but they had not the strength to win, and no foothold was left them in heaven. So the great dragon, whose name is Satan, was thrown down to the earth, and his angels with him.'

A most wonderful description of this fall is in Milton's *Paradise Lost*. We are not told the names of the guardians with flaming swords which turned every way, to keep the sinful Adam out of Eden. The main thing is to remember that belief in angels is very old, and that the name of Michael is a favourite among them, and will protect you if you have chosen it.

Nathaniel (Bartholomew)

On the face of it, Nathaniel and Bartholomew do not sound like the same name, but it is almost certain that they are. Bar means 'son of ', in the same way as Mac in Scots. Think of Simon Bar-Jonas, Bartimaeus the blind beggar, and others you can find in the Bible. Jesus' own name would be Jesus Bar-Joseph. Bartholomew, or Nathaniel, was the son of Tolmai and came from Cana, where the famous wedding was.

The day after Andrew and his brother Peter, both men of Bethsaida, had decided to follow Jesus, Jesus met Philip, who came from their town, and called him. Philip must have known Nathaniel, for as soon as he himself had decided to follow Jesus, he went to find Nathaniel (John 1, 45).

Nathaniel was sitting under a fig tree, out of the heat. When Philip came and said to him that they had found the man spoken of by Moses and the prophets, and that he came from Nazareth, Nathaniel said 'Nazareth! Can anything good come out of there?' Nazareth was known to be a poor place, with rough inhabitants; later they did not welcome Jesus when he returned there briefly.

'Come and see,' was all Philip replied. When Jesus saw

Nathaniel approaching, he said 'Here comes an Israelite without guile.' Nathaniel must have heard him.

'How do you know about me?' he asked. 'I saw you under the fig tree before Philip spoke to you,' Jesus answered.

It sounds like an ordinary conversation to us, but already Nathaniel knew that this Nazarene was somebody very unusual. 'Rabbi, you are the Son of God. You are the king of Israel,' was his answer. It was probably the only one he knew how to make. The kings of Israel, the anointed sons of God, were unforgotten by the Jewish people and it was always hoped one would come to redeem them from their present yoke under Herod and the Romans. However Jesus made no such claim, 'Because I saw you under the fig tree, do you say all that?' he replied. 'You shall see greater things,' and he went on to tell them some of these. He referred to himself not as Son of God, king of Israel, but as the Son of Man, who was the one foretold by the prophets, a far greater title.

We hear little more of Nathaniel, except that he was one of those who stayed with Jesus when many deserted him. With the others, he must have fled at the Crucifixion. After the Resurrection, he, Peter, Thomas and some of the rest got into a boat to fish, but caught nothing. A man standing on the shore called out to them to cast their nets on the other side. We know what happened; that the net was brought in full of fish, that Peter jumped into the water after John said it was Jesus, and later helped the rest to haul the net to land. Jesus had already lit a charcoal fire and cooked fish for their breakfast.

We know nothing more about Nathaniel for certain, though there are legends about his martyrdom. A hospital in London, and a massacre in France, were both named after him under his title of St. Bartholomew.

Nicholas

St. Nicholas' name suffers from the American version, Santa Claus. In fact he was not a cheery red-cheeked white-bearded old gentleman drawn by reindeer, but a bishop of Myra in the 4th century. He was one of the few Christian leaders to escape being put to death under Diocletian, who merely imprisoned him. He was released by the succeeding emperor, Constantine. His relics were taken to Bari, Apulia, in 1087.

Likenesses of him in icons all show a severe old man with grey or white hair, wearing a robe covered in small crosses. He is however known to have been devoted to children. He became the patron of youth, in particular scholars in the Middle Ages, and the schools celebrated his feast day, December 6th. This is the time when Christmas trees still appear in the shops, and the whole notion of commercial Christmas is tied up with this saint, which is not his fault. Up till last century, French children used to put their clogs, their sabots, outside the door on St. Nicholas' Eve, hoping to find them filled with sweets by the morning. Our Christmas stocking is the successor.

Who brought in the reindeer is uncertain, but Albert, Prince Consort, did *not* bring in the Christmas tree; this was done by the Russian Ambassadress, Princess Lieven, at a private dinner party in the reign of George IV. The next king, William IV, had a pleasant German queen who loved children as much as St. Nicholas had done, and she used to give Christmas parties for them at the Pavilion in Brighton, where there was a Christmas tree brought from her native forests of Meiningen. It was hung with gilded nuts and oranges, and there were presents for the children underneath. This was as early as 1832, long before Albert arrived in England. Sadly, none of Adelaide's own children lived, and she used to send presents of dolls and dolls' tea sets to little girls who had visited the dentist. There is no doubt that St. Nicholas would have approved of her.

His name was adopted by the Russian imperial family about the time of Napoleon. The Grand Duke Nicholas, later Tsar Nicholas I, was a very handsome man. He died in course of the Crimean War with Britain, where Florence Nightingale made the nursing profession famous. Nicholas II, who was murdered at the end of World War I with his family, was his great-grandson, the last of the Tsars.

Besides being the patron of scholars and youth, St. Nicholas is also the patron saint of sailors, travellers by sea and land, and thieves! He has suffered many things in the course of history.

St. Nicholas Owen was a clever old man who designed priests' hiding holes. Some of them have still not been discovered. In penal times he saved many lives in this way, at least for the time being; but he was caught and racked, although he suffered from a condition for which racking was illegal. He died in great agony, and was canonised as a saint in 1970.

He is still an excellent guardian of jewellery while you are away, if you pray to him.

The reason why the Scots call the devil Auld Nick is that during the Reformation they were taught not to respect Christmas, with which the name of St. Nicholas was already associated. You can show your respect for Christmas by remembering that it is the celebration of the birth of Christ, not entirely a matter of receiving presents; he was the best present of all.

Ninian

Ninian – Ringan, as he is affectionately known to the Scots – was born about 360. The place of his birth is said to be the one to which he later returned, south-west Scotland, the region of the Solway Firth. It is probable that Christian traditions persisted further north from the days of the Roman occupation and the building of Antonine's Wall (see article on St. Alban). Certainly Ninian was inspired to go to Rome and to have himself consecrated bishop by 394. He then visited the famous St. Martin at Tours in France, and made his way back to his homeland, having been commissioned to evangelise the south-west Scots and the Picts, who inhabited Galloway.

They were a wild lot, and for centuries regarded themselves as a separate kingdom, having crossed over in earlier times from Ireland; to this day the names in Galloway are different from those in mainland Scotland; McHaffie, McHarrie, McDouall, McCulloch. Their warriors were known by their eelskin sword-belts, and the women were as fierce as the men; one, a little later on than Ninian's time, took her own fleet of ships across the bay to kidnap a husband who had been refused her by his family, but was killed in the fighting.

Ninian landed in 397 on a pebbled shore near Whithorn, where there was a cave he at first lived in. By degrees his presence became known and he made converts, and was soon able to build a church, the first such building of stone, at Candida Casa, as Whithorn was named. Recently the foundations of the original chapel were identified and an archaeological dig goes on at the site, within view of the sea.

There is a pilgrimage every summer in honour of St. Ninian, along the pebbled shore to the cave, where Mass is said. To reach the shore it is a long walk through narrow paths, and until late years a hostile farmer used to walk his cows up and down the paths the night before the pilgrimage so that the going would be deep in mud! Nobody turned back, and the shore itself makes penitential walking over the deep pebbles to the cave. Inside there were, till lately, carved crosses in the soft stone, some from Ninian's time, but a few years ago vandals spoiled these and they are now protected by glass.

Crowds come to the annual pilgrimage, which is in July. One has to be early to get a seat on the rocks, or else climb up the steep cliff to where, among the green turf and blowing thrift with its dry pink flowers, tiny grasshoppers are tame. I have not seen such small ones elsewhere; they will perch on your arm. No doubt they were there in the time of Ninian; it is a remote spot, peaceful all the rest of the year.

The kings of Scots used, later on, to come down to Whithorn on pilgrimage, crossing a ford which can still be found in the river Cree, having walked all the way from Edinburgh. They knew that St. Ninian reached the Solway shores almost two hundred years before Augustine came to Canterbury. The last monarch to make the pilgrimage was Mary, Queen of Scots, during her six years' reign. She stayed at Clary, where the bishops of Galloway had a famous walled garden, and the water nearby is still called the Bishop's Burn. St. Ninian's well is on the old pilgrimage road across the moor, and is said never to run dry. He lived to be 72 years old, a great age in his day. Presently there was a convent at Wigtown, a church at Cruggleton, and signs everywhere that faith had taken root among this fierce people. It remains to this day.

Oliver

St. Oliver Plunkett is one of the Forty Martyrs canonised in 1970. He belongs especially to Ireland, where he was born in 1629.

He was an extremely handsome man, with fine dark eyes and the long curling hair of the period. He was educated by his uncle, a Benedictine abbot who later became archbishop of Armagh and Meath. Shortly, Oliver won an outstanding record at the Irish College in Rome. He went on to take degrees in canon and civil law, and became professor of theology and apologetics, but at the same time he worked with the Fathers of Charity among the very poor. This work was to stand him in good stead later on in his native land, where the poverty was appalling.

He returned to Ireland after 25 years, as its archbishop, having been consecrated in Ghent in 1669. This was necessary because of the times, which were hard on Catholics, though less so than they were to become. Charles II had lately been restored to the British throne, and was easy-going, unlike the Cromwellian government before him. Also, Charles had a Portuguese queen who was a Catholic, and Archbishop Plunkett spent a few days in London as the guest of her almoner. This would have been unthinkable either before then, or after.

Meantime, Archbishop Plunkett addressed himself to the many difficulties he found on arrival in Dublin. For one thing the Franciscans and Dominicans were at odds with one another, not a desirable state of affairs. The archbishop set out rules for the education and ordination of priests, tried to raise money for good causes, and got no thanks. He was accused of being on the side of the Tories, a word which in our day means a fairly respectable politician. In Plunkett's day it meant the wild Irish brigands whose property had been seized by the English under Cromwell, and who had taken to robbery as a way of life. In fact he ended by going to their hiding places to try to reform them, and also because, by then, open authority was made no longer possible.

In London, a dreadful man named Titus Oates had trumped up an anti-Catholic plot, something in the way the Gunpowder Plot had been thought up in a previous reign. Again it was stated that the Catholics were ready to murder the king, but the plot was really directed against his brother, the duke of York, who had become a Catholic convert. The queen, Catherine of Braganza, was also accused. Oates' lies were secretly supported by the earl of Shaftesbury, a fanatical opposer of all Catholics. Panic was whipped up among the people, and although Charles II saw through Titus Oates and in fact proved him a liar, it was too late to stop the wave of violence he had begun. All that happened to him was that he was put in the pillory, which meant having his hands secured in wood and being pelted with mud. Worse things by far happened to the victims of his lies.

In Ireland, soon no Catholic was permitted to enter the city of Dublin or any seaport. Archbishop Plunkett had to go into hiding and to say Mass secretly as in the old penal days. Meantime his uncle, who had brought him up, was dying and he visited him. Shortly after that he was arrested and taken to Dublin Castle, where he was left without means of contact with anyone for six weeks. At last he was allowed to visit a fellow-archbishop who was close to death, but everything he did and said was watched and reported.

There followed a trial like that of Christ. False informers were found, as then, and instead of accusing the prisoner of saying he could throw down the Temple, said he was plotting to bring a French army to overthrow the king.

Plunkett protested when his trial was moved to London; he knew there would be little chance of a fair hearing. Nevertheless the first trial came to no conclusion for lack of evidence. The archbishop was lodged in Newgate, a notorious prison, and the second trial, chiefly on the evidence of a perjured witness who was later hanged, found Oliver Plunkett guilty of high treason.

He was hanged, drawn and quartered at Tyburn on the first day of July, 1681. 'And being the first among the Irish, I will teach others, by the grace of God, by example, not to fear death.'

His head is in St. Peter's, Drogheda, recognisable as the man who is portrayed in a magnificent mosaic panel in Westminster Cathedral, showing him vested for Mass. On the Pope's visit to Ireland he brought the reliquary out into public view, and for an instant turned, so that it was possible for watchers in England to see again the face of St. Oliver Plunkett, archbishop and martyr.

Charles II became a Catholic on his deathbed in 1685. Doubtless the Irish martyr prayed for him.

Patrick

When anyone thinks of Ireland they think of St. Patrick. He is in the country's heart in a way that was never achieved in England by Augustine, in Galloway by Ninian, or even in the rest of Scotland by St. Columba or St. Margaret. Shamrocks – they are supposed not to take root anywhere else – were used by him to explain the Trinity. The fact that there are no snakes in Ireland is said to be because he banished them.

Times and seasons concerning him are confused, and this is Irish also. His birth is stated to have been in different places and at different dates; South Wales, Boulogne, Kilpatrick near Dumbarton; 373, 385, and his death in 461 or 463, or even in one statement 493, which would make him 120 years old! St. Columba, stated to be his sister's son, was not born till 60 years after Patrick's death, which would make a very young sister!

This apart, Patrick's father is known to have been a deacon named Calpurnius, so the boy was a Christian from the beginning. His Celtic name, perhaps a nickname, was Succat. When he was almost sixteen years old – this date is given as 389, work it out – he was captured by raiders, and carried off to slavery in Ireland. It is possible that he came to love the green land then. He was sold to a chief in Antrim whose name was Milchu.

Patrick escaped, may have been recaptured, but in the end got to France. There he became a monk, first at Tours – St Martin was the link between many of these early saints – and later at Lérins. At the age of 45 he was consecrated bishop. The earlier missionary St. Palladius having died meantime in Ireland, Pope Celestine sent Patrick there. There is even confusion about the place where he landed; some say it was Wicklow, others Strangford Lough in County Down. Certainly there is a town named Downpatrick there.

The first thing Patrick did was to journey to convert his old master Milchu. This shows his bravery. At Down he converted a chief with a similar name, Dichu. Dichu gave him some land. After that, Patrick went on to preach before the High King of Tara himself. He does not seem to have met with failure.

From there, he went to do penance at the place now famous as Croagh Patrick. Every year, and oftener than that, pilgrims make the ascent barefoot over its sharp stones. That is in Mayo, and Patrick thereafter went up and down the land, to Ulster and Cashel, north and south. He never failed to address the chiefs, knowing they had influence over their clans. Twenty years was spent by him in these journeyings, and legends grew. He had one bitter failure; several of his converts, including young girls, were carried off by raiders as he himself had been. Among these was a pagan British chief named Coroticus, to whom Patrick wrote a reproachful letter.

Growing old, he fixed his see at Armagh. The place of his death was however Saulpatrick, which means Patrick's barn; it was on some of the land Dichu had given him. Since then his very existence has been disputed, then reinstated; he is probably buried at Armagh. St. Patrick's Day is a day of great rejoicing both in Ireland and abroad, and Irish hostesses still send for bunches of shamrock and invite their Irish friends that day to tea. St. Patrick's bell, which he used at Mass, is in the Museum of Science and Art in Dublin.

Paul

Though I speak with the tongues of men and of angels, and have not charity, I am become as sounding brass, or a tinkling cymbal.

You will not find these exact words in your version of the Epistle to the Corinthians. For one thing, the word 'charity' has been replaced by the word 'love.' This is because a great many people thought of charity as merely a matter of giving old clothes they didn't want to the poor, which is not what St. Paul meant. The word he used, *caritas*, is perhaps best understood today by the term 'caring', although the media make use of this word far too much. Put in very modern terms indeed, what St. Paul meant to say was 'Although I may be able to to talk brilliantly on any subject, if I don't care what happens to other people I might as well keep quiet.'

However Paul, like Jesus, understood the beauty of language. Another modern alteration always seems to me a pity. *For now we see through a glass darkly, but then face to face* has been changed to 'through a mirror darkly' to make the meaning clearer to twentieth-century readers, because formerly it was not thought correct to refer to a mirror; the word used was looking-glass. However everyone now uses the word mirror, in the same way as we no longer call the radio the wireless; and one has to move with the times. All the same, if you know what a spondee is (if not, look up the dictionary) you will realise that a piece of poetic imagery has been lost with the new translation. Get hold of an old copy of the King James Bible, or the Doaui Bible, if you are interested enough, and study the differences.

Nevertheless St. Paul himself would certainly have wanted everyone to understand what he meant. He himself wrote that the Holy Spirit gives various gifts. His gifts were to preach and to write, rather than to work miracles, although he performed these and towards the end of his life, a cloth which had touched his skin was enough to cure sick persons if it was taken to them. Paul's mission, and he knew it, was to bring the news of Christ to the Gentiles, the non-Jewish races, the 'other sheep I have which are not of this fold' of which Christ had spoken.

This would be extraordinary enough, Paul himself having been born a Jew and reared a Pharisee; but well into young manhood he was a determined enemy of Christ and of the new sect who were not yet called Christians, and took a leading part in persecuting them.

Perhaps this can best be understood if we know that Saul of Tarsus, as he was then known (Paul is the Roman version of the name Saul, and his parents were Roman citizens like many subjects of the emperor) was a small man, who went bald early, and in addition had some physical disability, perhaps several. Like Moses, he stammered, and may have had a limp. He may also have been an epileptic. Certainly he used to pray all his life to have the affliction, whatever it was, removed, but it remained with him and in later years, he accepted it. As a young man, however, it probably made him aggressive to try to prove himself as good as taller, and healthier, boys and men. We can see this often today in people who have something wrong with them and think it matters more than it does. They often make a great deal of noise to attract attention to themselves, but if treated with understanding, calm down in the end.

Saul, as we must meantime call him, also had a brilliant mind. He was a pupil of the famous teacher Gamaliel, who however once got up and spoke out on behalf of the apostles (Acts 5, 37-39). Saul, on the other hand, was their enemy in the same way as the scribes and Pharisees had been enemies of Jesus. He no doubt heard from some of them about the carpenter from Nazareth who had had the impudence publicly to call them hypocrites and whited sepulchres, and had quite properly been executed shortly after by the authorities. There was a mistaken rumour that he had risen from the dead. Saul set himself to quench this rumour; the task made him feel important.

A young man named Stephen had meantime answered back in much the same fashion as Jesus himself had done, and Stephen was in charge of the new sect's finances, which they shared with one another. Stephen was captured, and taken out of the city to die by stoning. Those throwing stones laid their cloaks at Saul's feet; either he thought himself too important to throw stones in person, or else was physically delicate then.

What he saw of the way Stephen died did not change him all at once. After watching the first martyrdom he set out with renewed fury – those who know they are wrong are often furious – to harry the sect and enter their houses, casting both men and women into prison. Then he petitioned the authorities to let him go to Damascus, where the new religion was beginning to spread, to carry out the same things there.

On the journey to Damascus, the event happened that was to change Saul's life.

He had heard the dying Stephen say 'I can see heaven open, and the Son of Man seated at God's right hand.' Now, the Son of Man was of more importance by far than the term Son of God; the last was the title given to all anointed kings of Israel, among them Saul's own namesake of earlier times: but the Son of Man was the one who was promised from days of old by the prophets, who should be sent to redeem Israel.

The truth burst upon Saul like a blinding light; in a vision of Christ himself, seeing him as Stephen must have seen him. Saul heard a voice say 'Saul, Saul, why persecutest thou Me? It is hard for thee to kick against the pricks.' This last part, which Saul only referred to once in his life although he related the rest of the experience many times, means 'Stop deceiving yourself.'

Saul had fallen to the ground, and the men who were with him saw nothing, although they heard the voice. Perhaps, if Saul was an epileptic, they thought he was having one of his attacks; but when he got up at last he was blind. As a blind man he was led into Damascus, instead of coming in harm and anger; and stayed for three days unable to eat or drink, or to see.

Naturally the news got about, and a man named Ananias, who was a follower of Christ, had a vision also; he was told to go to the house where Saul was and to restore his sight. He did so, and 'the scales fell from his eyes' and he, Saul, was baptised. After that – he never did anything by halves – Saul became as zealous an apostle for Jesus Christ as he had hitherto been his enemy.

He began to preach in Damascus at once, inspired by the Holy Spirit. So successful was his preaching, and so many converts did he make, that he made enemies of the Jews. Thereafter they never ceased to be hostile and to try, wherever he might be found, to kill him. In the end, his converts let him down at dead of night over the city's walls in a basket, as the gates were being watched lest he go through. It was to be the first of many such adventures for the former respectable Pharisee.

In the meantime, he went back to Jerusalem. Not unnaturally the disciples there regarded him at first with suspicion, even thinking of him as a spy: the last they had heard of him had, after all, been as the man who guarded the cloaks while the rest stoned Stephen, and who had later thrown others among them into prison. It was as though, as somebody has said, Ian Paisley had announced his conversion to Rome! However one of them, named Barnabas, took Saul by the hand and brought him to them, telling them what he had heard of the preachings in Damascus and the number of converts made there. For a time Saul lived freely among them all in Jerusalem, but again the Jews plotted to murder him, and the disciples, hearing of this, themselves escorted him to Caesarea, seeing him off to Tarsus, his birthplace where he might be safe. We know that he had a sister, who at the time might have been living there though later she moved to Jerusalem.

Still it was not yet quite clear what he was to do. It was in fact St. Peter, not St. Paul (as Saul later become) who first baptised Gentiles (Acts 10, 47-48) at Joppa. Also, those who had fled at the death of Stephen preached in Carthage, Cyprus and Antioch, but to Jews only. Barnabus went to Antioch, accordingly, then when he had seen how things were there, journeyed to Tarsus to fetch Saul. The two men became close friends, and remained for a year in Antioch, which was a cool place surrounded by olive groves. Two other things happened there about then; the word 'Christian' was first used there, and Herod, arrayed on his throne to sit in judgment, began to writhe and died wretchedly, eaten up by worms. This was not the Herod of Christ's time, who had died in the same unpleasant way, but a successor, who had allowed himself, after the fashion of the Roman emperors, to be hailed as a god. We shall see that Paul, as he was beginning to be known, was to behave very differently under the same circumstances.

His journeyings took him to Cyprus, where he converted the governor. A sermon of his about then is remarkably like the speech made by Stephen before his accusers, and there is no doubt that the martyr was often in Paul's thoughts. He also healed a cripple, and like Stephen was stoned, but did not die of it. In fact he seemed to grow physically stronger the more that was asked of him.

To describe his unending journeys would take many pages, and you can read about them in the Book of Acts. For once, it is better to read these in modern translation, especially the description of the shipwreck which landed Paul at last on the island of Malta (where they have never forgotten him) on his way as a prisoner to Rome.

Before that, many things had happened to him. He had been described as 'a pest' by various authorities, had been flogged, imprisoned, put with his feet secured in the stocks (but an earthquake released him), stoned as above said, and on one occasion had been mistaken for the god Mercury, who was said to have had a ready tongue. The pagan priest – this was in Greece – had brought sacrificial oxen and garlands in Paul's honour; but Paul tore his garments, and said no god should be worshipped but the one the Athenians called the Unknown God, who needed no idols.

He caused riots wherever he went, notably in Ephesus, where he was accused of doing the silversmiths out of their living. They made statues and shrines to the goddess Diana, or Artemis, and bribed the crowds to shout down Paul, who was preaching in the amphitheatre. For two hours the crowd yelled 'Great is Diana of the Ephesians!' and it sounds even more menacing in Greek, *Megala hi Artemis Ephesio!* In such places Paul would shake out the folds of his cloak and leave, as Christ had taught the disciples to do; but he wrote many letters to the converts in Ephesus, also to his beloved Corinth, where he had stayed for eighteen months with his friends, Aquila and Priscilla, supporting himself – all Pharisees were taught a trade – by tentmaking out of goats' hair. On another occasion there was a rich woman named Lydia – she was a dye merchant, and probably employed slaves to gather the shellfish which gave Tyrian purple for cloaks – who was delighted to have Paul as her guest for as long as he cared to stay.

Otherwise, he is accused of being anti-feminist. It is true that his instructions to women today sound a trifle chauvinist. They were not to speak at meetings, should keep their hair covered, must on no account drink too much wine, and must obey their husbands. In fact Paul told everyone to take a little wine for the stomach's sake, and in literal translation the word 'obey' means 'give ear to', which is not an unreasonable request! It must be remembered also that Paul was a Jew, and Jewish women are subservient, in some sects to this day. Moreover the wives and daughters of Roman emperors set such a bad example of misused power – the wife of Claudius was one of the worst, and very proud of her long curling hair – that no doubt Paul, who had suffered many things from so-called influential women (we have all met them) resented the enormously high headdresses of false hair which were then fashionable among these ladies. His influence was such that for centuries women's hair remained unseen in Christian countries. He had meantime had his own, or what there was of it, cut because of a vow.

He had spoken before Agrippa, who was Herod's successor, so movingly that the king said, 'Almost thou persuadest me to be a Christian'. However the governor, whose name was Festus, merely said to Paul, 'Much learning hath made thee mad.' Paul, in the end, as the Roman citizen he was, appealed to Caesar. This was to prove his death-warrant.

He was taken to Rome after the Malta shipwreck, and lived there in a form of house arrest for two years, during which he was free to write to his friends and entertain them. Among his last words are *I have fought the good fight, I have finished the course, I have kept the faith*. No one kept it better; and although he and St. Peter did not agree, both of them being leaders and strong personalities, they are buried together in the tomb at Rome, as befits the two men who strove greatly to establish the Church in the world, and both of whom gave their lives for Christ. St. Paul died by the sword in the reign of Nero. His feast day, and St. Peter's, is on June 29th.

Peter

Jesus liked to play on words. It is probable that he knew Greek as well as Aramaic, the language which was spoken in Palestine. The most famous instance of this is the way he changed Simon into Peter.

Simon, the son of Jonas, was a native of Bethsaida. He had a brother Andrew (see our article) and the pair of them shared a house in Capernaum by the lakeside, where they were fishermen. In the house also lived Simon's wife, who later accompanied him on his travels and is mentioned by St. Paul, and her mother. It was a small house (it is still there) and conditions must have been cramped. Nevertheless the two brothers were out fishing most of the day with their partners, James and John.

Simon was first led to follow Jesus by his brother Andrew, after they had been together to hear John the Baptist preach. A man was baptised whom they did not know, and they heard the Baptist say that he himself was not worthy to untie the fastening of this man's sandals, and that he was the Lamb of God. At that, Andrew fetched Simon and both brothers followed Jesus to where he lived. They talked together for a long time.

After that, John the Baptist was arrested and imprisoned. The fame of Jesus began to spread instead, and when he walked by the lakeside at Capernaum Simon and Andrew were out in their boat casting their nets, but left them and followed him. So did James and John, who had been on shore mending their nets. It is like Simon Peter to have been out on the water first; later on he always did everything first, sometimes getting into trouble. He was an impulsive person and a natural leader. Jesus saw both qualities, and knew that when his own task was accomplished this was the man to take over. However meantime several things had to be put right.

Soon, like others, Simon realised that Jesus was the Son of Man, the Christ who would come and save Israel as the prophets had foretold. He did not yet know that more than Israel was to be saved, and that he himself would be the first to preach to the Gentiles after a vision. All he knew, and must have been puzzled though pleased, was that Jesus told him he was Kepha, which is Aramaic for rock: the Greek form is Cephas, and Petros, like the French Pierre and the Latin Petrus, is the fuller translation. *Tu es Petrus* is the hymn sung on entry by the Pope into St. Peter's, Rome. Peter was chosen to witness the Transfiguration, but misunderstood it and wanted to build three tents.

He was in fact still very far from being a rock. Only a little after receiving his new name he blurted out that Jesus should by no means die as he had said. Jesus turned on him. 'Get behind me, Satan.' Jesus had known Satan of old, had seen him fall like lightning from the sky, had met him in the wilderness. He knew that Peter could be tempted as he had himself been. Jesus knew that he had come to die for men, but that by his own power he could avert this. It was unhelpful to have Peter remind him of the fact. However it is understandable that Peter and the rest were bewildered at what seemed like a change of face.

Peter came to understand his own weaknesses, especially after he had boasted that he would never betray Christ even if all the rest did. The steps can still be seen where he stood and saw Jesus regarding him after the cock had crowed thrice. He 'went out', and wept bitterly. Ashamed of himself, as well as being afraid like the rest, he was not at the foot of the Cross like John. He had fallen asleep at Gethsemane when Christ needed him; he had angrily cut off the ear of the high priest's servant as Jesus was arrested, as though to try and prove that he himself could be of some use after all. 'Those who take the sword shall perish by the sword,' Christ said, in the midst of the betrayal. Earlier, we read how Peter at first refused to have his feet washed by Jesus, then when he realised he was wrong said 'Lord, not my feet only, but my hands and my head.' This is typical of the way he never did things halfway; when he repented, it was wholeheartedly. Although his faith was not yet strong enough to bear the walking on water alone (how like Peter to leap first out of the boat on two occasions, and to go right into the empty tomb!) he became, after receiving the Spirit at Pentecost, a wise leader, fit for the gift Christ had made him of the power to loose and to bind.

It is true that the two Epistles written in his name may not be his, but he is almost certainly the inspiration for the Gospel of Mark, who became his secretary. It was to Mark's mother's house in Jerusalem that Peter went after his miraculous release from prison, when the chains were struck from his feet and the gates flung open. The maid – we know her name was Rhoda – ran to tell everyone in the house Peter was standing outside in the street, and nobody believed her. It is interesting to remember that Peter did not, after that, enter the house, but went off to a place by himself. He had thought the whole thing was a dream, and like Christ had to be alone to pray.

He became able to work miracles and cures, and had the vision of strange meats let down on a cloth, to tell him his mission was to the Gentiles also. You can read all about it in the Book of Acts, also Peter's speech on the election of a new man to replace Judas among the twelve. He preached to the Gentiles before St. Paul, with whom he never got on; two born leaders seldom do. However he had seen Christ's promise come true; he had become a fisher of men. He may have remembered, and smiled at it, the time Jesus had told him to go and catch a fish with a coin in its mouth to pay the temple tax for both of them.

He was crucified at Rome in the reign of Nero. His last well-meant impulse was to ask that this should be done upside down. He was not to know that this would make death come more quickly. It had only been that he did not want to presume to die in exactly the same way as his Master.

Philip

St. Philip was one of the apostles. He brought Nathaniel to Jesus, saying he had found the one about whom Moses had written and the prophets taught. Later he brought Gentiles to Jesus, a daring step for a Jew. He was a forthright, enthusiastic person with perhaps not enough time for thought; Jesus once said to him 'Have you known me all this time, Philip, and do not understand that if you have seen me, you have seen the Father?' But Philip was only one of those who found this difficult to understand. It is a mystery, a matter of faith. Once the evidence of the Resurrection was before him, Philip, like Thomas, no doubt believed; the miracle of the loaves and fishes had not been enough for him; how could 5,000 be fed?

It may be the same Philip or a different one who baptised the Ethiopian in Acts 8. There is a Gospel of Philip which is not thought to have been written by the apostle, and it contains stories about Jesus which are not in Scripture. Nevertheless his name was used by dukes of Burgundy and kings of France, later on of Spain; and the next saint, St. Philip Howard, we know a great deal more about than his predecessor, for he lived much nearer our time and most of what he did has been recorded.

Everyone thought Philip Howard had been born with a golden spoon in his mouth in 1557. His father was the Duke of Norfolk, his young mother the heiress of Arundel, and he was the first son. He was also the godchild of King Philip II, husband of Queen Mary Tudor. At his grand christening the king himself held him at the font.

However things began to go wrong at once, apart from the king's departure to his wars abroad and the queen's death of a broken heart, so that her half-sister Elizabeth ascended the

English throne. Before that, Philip's young mother had died of a fever when he was less than a month old. His father, who was only 19, married again three times. One of the marriages, to a widow with children, brought Philip his own wife Anne Dacre, who was his stepsister. Anne was heiress of more lands in the north. She was a beautiful, pious and scholarly girl, but for a long time Philip did not love her. Meantime his father the Duke made a fatal plan to marry yet again, to the imprisoned Mary, Queen of Scots. The plot was discovered, and Norfolk was executed and his ducal title forfeit. Philip was never a duke, therefore, but as earl of Arundel he had lands, money and titles. He became a favourite of the queen.

Elizabeth is one of the best remembered women in history. She was a scholar, witty and practical, but intensely vain. She could not bear her courtiers to admire any woman but herself, and those who did, fell from favour. For a long time Philip behaved as expected, flattering and amusing the Queen and keeping on good terms with her powerful minister Cecil, who had been appointed his guardian as a boy. Moreover, Elizabeth, who only saw Anne once in her life, hated her for the rest of it, as the story will show.

Gradually, both Anne and Philip, in their separate ways, became attracted to the forbidden and persecuted Catholic Church. It suited Elizabeth to be its enemy. For one thing the Pope, St. Pius V, had recently excommunicated her and had released her subjects from their allegiance. This was unwise, at least to us with hindsight, as many English chose to support the queen against the Pope, who was a long way off and had not been obeyed for over a generation except in the time of the late Queen Mary. English Catholics were fined and imprisoned, and if a priest was found he was condemned to a prolonged and terrible death.

At this dangerous time, Anne was received into the Church. She did not tell her husband, whom she loved but seldom saw. On the other hand, Philip himself, without telling Anne, had been deeply impressed by the answers of Father Edmund Campion, S.J., who had been betrayed, imprisoned, tortured, then made to appear before the court. The more Philip thought of it the more he realised Campion had been right and all the rest, himself included, wrong. By then, the priest had gone to his martyr's death at Tyburn.

Unlike Anne, Philip had no privacy; his every move was noted, and in his official position he had to accompany the Queen to her new Church of England services and recognise her as its head. For some time he used to slip into the side aisles or even feign illness, but of course this was observed. No one at Court, or in the country, was unobserved; there was Cecil, who paid spies, and Walsingham, with spies and counter-spies; and Philip was the son of the man who had aspired to the queen of Scots, Elizabeth's rival for the throne, and a Catholic. Philip began to be suspected.

It was about then that he realised that he loved his wife. They were both in their mid-twenties and had been married at twelve years old. Anne had always loved him, and for a time they were happy together. Then the jealous Queen had Anne, who was expecting a child, arrested. She was kept without liberty, or permission to see her husband, for a year. During this time she gave birth to a daughter. It was suggested that if the child were christened Elizabeth it might placate the Queen. This was done, much against Anne's will; but she was released shortly, and Philip rode joyfully to bring his wife and child home.

This was of course reported, and he was in lessening favour; the net began to close in.

Campion had revived Catholicism in England by his presence and by his death. It would never again be in danger of extinction, and, lacking Campion himself, it needed a leader. Philip Howard gladly offered himself for this post. He got in touch with Dr Allen, the Superior at Douai, overseas. His letters were intercepted and read, and one was forged as being from Dr Allen, advising him to leave England.

He bade farewell unwillingly to his wife, his little daughter and, as he thought, his country. Anne was expecting a second child, and they both hoped for a son. It was a bitter time to have to leave, but Philip thought he was obeying orders. Once out at sea, he saw he had been mistaken. A small ship of war drew up alongside and he was taken prisoner, and brought back to be lodged in the Tower of London.

The queen herself, as a young girl, had been a prisoner in the Tower, and only her cool head had saved her life. She knew exactly what it felt like; but Philip was put in the worst place there was, the Beauchamp Tower, above a stinking drain. Its smell was so dreadful those above it fell ill, and although the Earl of Arundel was used to servants, and his servants were devoted to him and were eventually allowed to come to him, not one could stay. He nursed several through illnesses, then was left alone; except for his dog, which Anne had sent him. However she was not allowed to visit him or to write, and for a long time he had no news of her and was afraid she had died at the second birth. This was the worst part of his imprisonment.

The queen then did a cruel thing. She allowed word to be sent that the countess of Arundel had given birth to another daughter. In fact Anne had produced a fine son. Elizabeth hoped that Philip Howard would be so desperate at the news that he would forswear his religion in order to be set free. She was wrong. From then on Philip grew ever more steadfast in his faith, although till then he had hardly received the Sacrament, and was only to be able to do so for a very short period, supposedly in secret. Meantime, in the end word was sent to him that he had a son, an heir he was never to see.

He was three times removed from his noisome lodging. Once he was ordered to be fined £10,000 and to be detained at the queen's pleasure. On a second occasion he was moved to the Lanthorn Tower, and it was here that he was able to make the acquaintance of an old priest, Father Bennet, who said Mass for Philip and a few others. Philip, earl of Arundel, served at Mass.

Philip

It was about the time of the queen of Scots' execution; Philip of Spain was preparing the Armada as a result; and every action of the Catholics in the Tower was watched and reported. They were accused of having Mass said for a Spanish victory; they had been put in the Lanthorn Tower because it contained arms and cannon and they could be said to be conducting a siege. Poor old Father Bennet was tortured on the rack, and admitted several things which had never happened; not all priests, or all men, were as heroic as Campion.

Philip was heroic in a different way. For a long time, after being brought before the Star Chamber and condemned for treason, he daily expected to be led out to die. That Elizabeth and Cecil did not go to these lengths is probably because the earl of Arundel was greatly beloved; while he was free to walk on the leads of the roof with a gaoler, crowds had gathered below to watch and see him. Also, Elizabeth may have remembered the handsome young courtier he had been.

His appearance had changed. At first he had been handsome, it is true, but it is an arrogant face in early portraits. The last one of all, which Anne persuaded them to let her have painted of him in prison, shows a humble man with shining eyes, his head shaven. It is not an unhappy face, despite all that had happened to him and that he knew was happening to his wife.

Anne had been treated abominably, her house broken into, her goods and money taken; in the end, the queen allowed her £8 a month, but it was not regularly paid. Nevertheless she somehow managed to do a great deal of good to the poor, walking for miles when they had taken away her coach, visiting beggar women in childbirth, helping and comforting them. At the same time she was in constant fear for Philip; she must have heard that one of his questioners had exclaimed 'I will hang you myself!' Nevertheless the night before the earl's trial, she heard, for the first and last time, a nightingale sing in the garden in London, and knew that he would not be executed despite the verdict of guilty passed by the Star Chamber and, later, a public hearing.

They never met again. Philip died after eleven years in the Tower, probably from the effects of the stinking drain. His knees had turned black with hours of kneeling in prayer; he daily said a rosary Anne had contrived to send him. When she heard that he was dead, she fell into so long a swoon that it was thought she had died herself; but she lived on into old age, dispensing much charity. Towards the end of her life, back at Arundel, she used, on her grandchildren's birthdays, to send for the poor children of the village and give each child a slice of plum cake and a penny for each year of the grandchild's age.

St. Philip Howard was canonised among the Forty Martyrs of England and Wales in 1970. His bones were removed from the Tower to Arundel, then much later to the cathedral there, named after him. His statue stands smiling above the altar, with one hand on the collar of his dog.

Rupert

Salzburg is a small town through which a river runs and amazing mountains can be seen beyond. It was an archbishopric under Charlemagne, who was crowned emperor at Rome in 800; but one of its earliest bishops, Rupert, was descended from more ancient kings, the Merovings, who ruled the Franks, and among whom was St. Dagobert, who chose Paris as his capital and built the abbey of St Denis.

Knowing some of this, the duke of Bavaria sent for Rupert to ask him to found a mission in Salzburg. It was still at that time known by its Roman name of Juvavum, and its people were the Rhaeto-Romans. It is probably due to the new bishop Rupert that the town's name became Salzburg, the city of salt; he was the first to encourage mining there, and is usually shown holding a barrel of salt.

He brought a community of Irish Celtic monks to found a monastery and church to St. Peter. Ireland was at that time a stronghold of Christianity, as at the coming of the Saxons many Celts had fled there. The church of Sankt Peter is still in Salzburg. Nearby, Rupert also founded a convent at Nonnberg with his niece, Ehrentrude, as its first abbess. It was already 200 years since St. Benedict had founded his monastic order, and soon both these foundations became Benedictine on the orders of Pope Boniface.

Rupert had meantime founded another church over the grave of a very early saint, Maximilian, after whom later emperors were often named. He travelled a great deal, visiting places such as Lorch and Wallensee which now have other names; all this was in the eighth century, and a great deal has altered since. However St. Rupert and his barrel of salt are still to be seen in Austrian churches. A famous one in Salzburg itself is dedicated to him.

He himself dedicated the city of Salzburg to the great St. Martin of Tours, making the latter patron of the Franks and Merovings. The latter dynasty did not however survive, and that of the Carolingians took its place. The greatest of them was Charlemagne himself.

Rupert had died in 718, and was buried in Sankt Peter. However in 773 his remains were translated to his own named cathedral by a subsequent bishop of Salzburg, still an Irishman; St. Virgil the Geographer (see our article). St. Rupert was invoked for a long time in cases of erysipelas and children's convulsions, but luckily neither of these is now as common as used to be the case. Prince Rupert of the Rhine was named after the saint, and an Order of Knights of St. Rupert flourished from 1701 till 1805.

Christ said how important salt was, and St. Rupert can be remembered for his encouragement of the mines. They made

Salzburg rich, and it is now so popular a place to live that houses are difficult to find. Mozart was a native of the city, and served for a time under a much less pleasant archbishop than St. Rupert, being finally kicked downstairs!

Sebastian

Saint Sebastian is familiar to us from many paintings which show him pierced with arrows. In a remote part of Austria I came on the legend that he was afterwards drowned in a drain. This is very interesting, as it happened; but is not generally known about although Butler, in his *Lives of the Saints*, mentions it. It was the final punishment accorded by the emperor Diocletian.

Sebastian was born in the third century, of Milanese parents who were probably Christian. Milan is so named because in those days, under the Roman emperors, its name was Mediolanum, midway between the north of the empire and the south.

Sebastian joined the Roman army in 283 for a curious reason. He had no wish to be a soldier, because he hated killing; but he thought that, in a time of great persecution, he could help as many of his fellow-Christians as possible from a position in the army. He was soon able to persuade two martyrs to persevere in their deaths despite the pleas of their friends that they recant and save their lives. Later he cured their bereaved old father of gout, and comforted him.

He made many other cures, including that of a woman named Zoë who for six years had been deprived of speech. Sebastian made the sign of the cross on her tongue and it was loosed. Poor Zoë had not long in which to talk; she was hung up by the heels by the authorities, and smoked to death over a bonfire. Appalling tortures of this and other kinds were meted out by Diocletian, or rather by his subordinate Galerius.

Sebastian seems to have made a good officer, and the emperor noticed him and found him agreeable company. He decreed that the young Milanese should be in constant attendance on his own person. Perhaps Sebastian hoped to be able in this way to help his fellow-Christians even more: but when he refused to deny his faith, the order was given that he be shot to death with arrows. This was done, and he suffered the agony shown in so many paintings.

Nevertheless he was not dead. Later a widow named Irene found the dreadfully wounded man alive, took him to her house and nursed him back to health. However Sebastian refused to hide himself or to try to escape. He preferred to confront the emperor. Perhaps he still hoped to convert Diocletian. He awaited him on a certain staircase where he was known to pass by. When he came, Sebastian informed him of his wickedness.

It was hardly the best way to save his own life. It is true that the sight of the man he had supposed to be dead amazed Diocletian for moments. However he recovered, and ordered the young man to be clubbed to death and his body thrown into the common sewer.

The order was carried out, and this time Sebastian died. A woman named Lucina had a vision of the body's whereabouts, found it, and conveyed it to secret burial in the catacombs, where the early Christians held their hidden meetings. The place is supposed to be near the saint's basilica, on the Appian Way.

Saint Sebastian is the patron saint of archers, soldiers and the plague. There is a relic of him in Westminster Cathedral in London. His name was long a favourite choice, and one of the most famous owners of it was Johann Sebastian Bach. The saint's feast day is January 22nd.

Stephen

Everyone has heard of St. Stephen as the first martyr, but less notice is taken of his life than of his death by stoning.

A martyr is described in the dictionary as 'a person who undergoes death or suffering for any great cause.' It is a term usually applied to the Christian faith, and hundreds of martyrs have been inspired by the example of Stephen and some, like him, have been declared saints.

What is a saint? Again, the dictionary: someone 'having won by exceptional holiness a high place in heaven and veneration on earth.' To be canonised by the Church is to be officially recognised as one, but there are many people we know who in their daily lives can be described as saints, who will probably never be remembered, let alone canonised. On the other hand, some have been canonised whom we do not all necessarily think of as saintly. However Stephen, in his life and death, was most certainly a saint.

He was one of the seven deacons appointed by the apostles in order to leave them free from worldly matters. The details will be found in Acts 6. Also, it is mentioned that Stephen in particular was 'a man full of grace and power,' 'a man full of faith and the Holy Spirit.' After the apostles had laid their hands on him (this may mean that he was ordained), he was put in charge of the finances of the growing community, which was not yet known as Christian.

This meant that Stephen had to be scrupulously fair and honest. It also probably means that he was chosen for his tact. Money and possessions were shared equally among the group, and anyone who has such a job today knows the squabbles that can arise if anybody thinks they have been short-changed. There were no complaints about Stephen.

Stephen

Also, he was said to work signs and miracles among the people. The regard in which he was held, and the way they relied on him, is shown by the numbers who fled abroad after his death. Even this, however, had its good side; the news of the Gospel was spread early in far parts, such as Antioch, from which one of the seven deacons had originally come. His name was Nicholas and he was a converted Jew. The fact that there were a growing number of these alarmed the authorities, who hoped they had got rid of Jesus of Nazareth by crucifying him.

Among the most ruthless persecutors of the new sect was a young Pharisee named Saul of Tarsus. We do not know, but it is probable that it was he who set on foot the hunt for Stephen. Presently he was to become known for casting men and women into prison and raiding their houses if they were suspected of being followers of Christ (see article on Paul).

Stephen knew they were after him, and there is a tradition that for a long time there stood a tree into which he climbed to hide from his pursuers. This was not cowardice but common sense; he was of use to the community. Nevertheless they found him, dragged him down and took him before the Sanhedrin, where exactly as in the case of Jesus they had bribed false witnesses to say that Stephen had blasphemed the law of Moses.

Stephen replied with a brilliant speech, which you can still read in Acts 6, relating the whole history of God and man from the time of the promise to Abraham and the appearances to Moses, the history of the Jewish people, and the way they had betrayed both God and Moses by their late treatment of God's own son. All of them fixed their eyes on Stephen 'and his face appeared to them like the face of an angel.'

However when Stephen said he saw heaven open, and the Son of Man, Christ the Messiah, seated at the right hand of God, they stopped their ears, shouted and rushed him out of the city. There they laid their cloaks at the feet of Saul, and proceeded to stone Stephen to death. Death by stoning is slow and painful. Near the end Stephen sank to his knees. As Christ had done, he begged God not to hold this sin to their charge. Then 'he fell asleep.'

Certain devout men, it is said, buried the body with great mourning. It must have been thought, as it had been thought after Christ was crucified, that this was the end of everything. Many fled, as had been stated. For a time Saul of Tarsus busied himself by punishing everyone by imprisonment he could find. There is no doubt that the death of Stephen had made an impression on his mind that he preferred to blot out for the time. Later, on his way to Damascus to do more harm, he had a vision on the road. Soon he had become Paul the apostle.

It often happens that a martyr's death has tremendous effects on those who see it; countless instances can be related through history. Stephen will always be remembered as having begun it all. The ancient carol 'On the feast of Stephen' refers to the day after Christmas, December 26th.

Thomas

There are several saints of the name of Thomas, and although they lived at different times and in different ways they had one quality in common. All of them were stubborn men.

This can be a virtue if it means standing by what you know to be right. It can be a fault if you stick to an opinion merely because you are the one who thought of it.

The earliest of the name, after whom the rest were probably called, is the apostle Thomas, one of the twelve chosen by Jesus to carry on his ministry. Most of these men were rough diamonds, but possessed special qualities Jesus saw at the beginning. Thomas is mentioned three times in this way in the first three Gospels, usually alongside Matthew the former tax collector. We know that Thomas was a twin, because he is also called Didymus, but there is no mention of the twin brother or sister.

Thomas's stubbornness made him refuse to believe in what the others told him, that Christ had risen from the dead. 'Unless I put my hands in the prints of the nails, and into the wound in his side, I will not believe,' he said. Nevertheless when Christ appeared and invited him to do so, there was no need. Thomas believed fervently, and from being Doubting Thomas became Thomas the apostle, present on the first day of Pentecost and also in Acts 1, where Peter spoke of the need to cast lots to replace Judas Iscariot. Later Thomas seems to have travelled widely on his missions; we hear of him in India, and one version says he was martyred there; another says he went to Parthia and is buried in Edessa, where the Shroud was hidden for long. St. Thomas is the patron saint of Portugal.

Another very stubborn man indeed was St. Thomas Aquinas, born in 1225 and described as the finest of Christian thinkers. He had to contend with an ambitious family, who had decided that he was to become abbot of Monte Cassino, the famous Benedictine foundation. However Thomas did not want to be a Benedictine but, to his family's horror, a preaching friar, a Dominican. In those early days friars were considered hardly respectable, and Thomas's family kidnapped him and shut him up for almost two years in one of their castles. Freed at last, he went to study at Cologne under the great teacher Albertus Magnus. Thomas however was so busy thinking that he seldom spoke, and as he was also extremely large his fellow-students mocked at him and called him the Dumb Ox. 'One day the bellowing of that ox will be heard throughout the world,' said his teacher, and this has come true. St. Thomas Aquinas – he died in 1274 – has written thoughts and ideas about the nature of God which in the first place shocked certain people but are now accepted as profound and true thought. His *Summa Theologica* is his most famous document, but he also wrote the marvellous Latin prayers we know, *Pange*

Lingua Gloriosa, *Adoro Te Devote*, and many others. At the end of his life he stopped writing. 'All I have written seems nothing but straw,' he said. He had come to a closer vision of God than even he could put into readable form.

The third saint is quite equally stubborn, and was killed for it. Thomas Becket was the son of humble parents, who made his way by the brilliance of his mind. He became a friend of the king of England, Henry II, and presently his chancellor. Thomas went in a splendid embassy to Paris to try to arrange the betrothal of the king's son, aged eight, to the king of France's daughter, aged three. When the folk of Paris saw the magnificent embassy – there were even monkeys riding on horses, great mastiffs walking as guards, and barrels of English beer for everyone – they said how great a king this must be who could send so rich an embassy, and sent the little three-year-old bride across the Channel at once. Thomas also gave grand dinners in London, and the king, who liked to make fun of his friend, used to ride his horse into the spick-and-span hall, dismount and leap across the table still dirty from hunting, and sit down to eat uninvited. Henry II was a man who never stood on ceremony, and was known as Curtmantle because of the short cloak he wore. He never wore gloves and, after the coronation, refused to wear his crown. He was a great lawgiver and firm ruler, but could be treacherous. He also made the mistake of thinking that Thomas would obey him whether he was right or wrong.

Shortly he decided that, as he himself had to be in Normandy a great deal, he would leave Thomas to govern England under his orders as chancellor and, also, as archbishop of Canterbury. It was what we now call a package deal, but what Henry had not taken into account was that Thomas liked to do one thing at a time and to do it as well as he could. On accepting, after some hesitation, the archbishopric, he had himself ordained and, at the same time, sent back the chancellor's seal to King Henry in Normandy. Henry was furious, as it ruined his plans. He also may already have had a personal grudge against Thomas Becket. Henry's young brother William had greatly loved a rich young English widow who owned broad lands in her own right. It was advisable to keep these lands in the king's family, as otherwise a troublesome baron might marry the lady. However Thomas Becket discovered that the two lovers were closely related, and caused the Pope to forbid the marriage. Young William died of a broken heart at Rouen, and the king married the lovely widow to his half-brother instead. However when Archbishop Becket was later murdered, one of the murderers hacked with his sword and shouted 'That for the king's brother William!' so it must have been remembered.

Meantime, Thomas Becket had greatly altered his way of living. Although his life had always been personally pure, he now abandoned all outward show except for what belonged to the Church. His processions were magnificent and he wore gorgeous copes and mitres in the famous *opus Anglicanum* embroidery, but beneath he wore a hair shirt invaded with lice. He practised other penances and was almost a different man from the one who had ridden in the great embassy, given the great feasts, and had accompanied Henry to the siege of Toulouse with an army and brazen trumpets, making more clamour than anybody. In a way one might say that he was an actor who threw himself wholly into his part, whatever it might be.

He and the king fell out mostly over a clause in the laws of England as Henry wanted them made, namely that clerics convicted of a crime should then be turned over to the civil court. Henry had reasons, for in practical fact many criminals got off very lightly as it was, if they were clerics; they were punished by the episcopal courts, which meant prison at the bishops' expense, and naturally the bishops did not want to make the sentences too long as it meant spending their money on the prisoners' keep. However Archbishop Becket held out for the principle that religious persons were not subject to the king. You may agree or you may not; but at a great meeting held at Clarendon, Henry perjured himself by altering a document Thomas had at last agreed to sign. Thomas refused to sign it, and after that it was war between the two men. Thomas eventually escaped to France, where the king there made him welcome. Nevertheless for six years he was in extreme poverty, as Henry withheld his income.

In the end, when matters appeared to have reached an impasse, the quick-tempered Henry was heard to say one day at a feast at Bures, his hunting-lodge near Bayeux (four hundred oaks had been felled to build it), 'Is this low-born clerk to get the better of me?' The speech is often misreported; the words 'turbulent priest' were not used; Henry, in his way, was a devout Christian, though with an eye to the main chance. On hearing the words, four men slipped out of the hall.

Becket meantime had returned to England, and had been greeted with insults from the nobles but great joy from the people of Canterbury, who rang all the bells in his honour and decked the town's streets. He said Mass on Christmas Day, but on the day following was murdered in front of his own altar by the four men who had come from Bayeux. They went away, and came back later to do more harm to the dead body; but the horrified monks had already placed it in a tomb.

The tomb began to be famous; there were miracles at it. In time, it was to become one of the richest in Christendom. The king hid in Ireland until the shock and anger at the murder should have died down. Later, though he was not directly responsible for the murder, he did public penance, barefoot and scourged by eighteen monks and five prelates. Next day, a token of St. Thomas's forgiveness was brought to him; news of the capture of the king of Scots.

This king, William the Lion, had invaded England from the north, and there were other invasions at the same time which, had they been successful, would have taken Henry's kingdom from him. Now, William the Lion was taken to Falaise in

Normandy and made to sign a treaty making Scotland Henry's vassal. He had been taken prisoner at the lifting of a mist in Northumbria which was said to be due to the intervention of St. Thomas. When King William was released, he went back to Scotland and built an abbey in honour of the saint, at Arbroath, and is buried there. Perhaps Thomas interceded for Scotland also, as in the next reign her freedom was bought back with money used for Richard the Lion Heart's crusade.

All down the centuries pilgrimages were made to the tomb at Canterbury, by then covered with rich jewels. In Henry II's own reign the king of France, after three visions of St. Thomas, came to pray for the recovery of his only son, who was ill. (The son recovered, to become a considerable thorn in the sides of the later kings of England.) An even more famous pilgrimage is the one described in Chaucer's *Canterbury Tales*. St. Thomas Becket had by then replaced St. Edward the Confessor as England's favourite saint.

All went well in this way till the reign of Henry VIII, who in 1538 ordered Becket's tomb to be destroyed and his bones powdered and thrown in the River Stour. This was because Becket in his day had defied the authority of a king, and Henry VIII had begun to fancy himself as head of the Church in England. However his orders do not seem to have been carried out; at Angers, the old capital of Henry II in Anjou, there are some of the relics, and a series of windows showing the martyrdom. It is as though the two former friends, archbishop and king, were reconciled at last.

Timothy

Timothy was the companion of St. Paul. Two famous epistles are addressed to him. He was the son of a Greek father and a Jewish mother named Eunice, who may have been a Christian. Timothy himself was converted by Paul at Lystra. He joined the apostle on his second missionary journey, and they became great friends although Paul was much older; Timothy was almost like his son. He became entrusted by Paul with various important commissions among the new churches, a task which demanded knowledge and tact. Later he shared Paul's imprisonment at Rome.

He was left in full charge of the church at Ephesus, an important place to which it is said Our Lady was taken by St. John. The streets were swept with water daily and it was a rich and cultured city to which, as you know, Paul wrote the Epistle to the Ephesians. Timothy himself is said to have been martyred there later. He has three feast days according to the different branches of the Christian Church; January 22nd for the Greek Orthodox, January 23rd for the Coptic, and January 24th for the Latin. All this shows that he was greatly venerated, and that, like many people of whom we do not know much, he got quietly on with the task assigned to him after the apostle's death. You may still see, in Ephesus, a fish carved in the stone of the street for a Christian symbol, with in Greek the anagram (look it up) for 'Jesus Christ, God's Son our Saviour'. Possibly the carving is as old as Timothy's time. A fish was the secret symbol of the faith before it was possible to use the crucifix. See if you can think of reasons why a fish should have been chosen.

Virgil

You will probably have heard of Virgil the poet, in classical times; he wrote the *Eclogues*, the *Georgics* and the *Aeneid*, including much practical advice about how to look after olives, vines and bees. Dante chose him as his guide through the underworld in *The Inferno*. However it is less well known that a Christian writer of the seventh century disguised himself under the same name and invented a fifth kind of Latin out of four varieties he said he had discovered.

There was certainly a St. Virgil as well. On a recent visit to Salzburg, in Austria, I stayed at the St. Virgil Centre, in the middle of a pleasant park. On the wall of the entrance, I noticed a large bronze figure in the act of being borne up to heaven, lacking a right arm and right eye. I was told that this was St. Virgil, and assumed that he was one of the unlucky bishops who had suffered mutilation under the last pagan emperors before Constantine, who mocked Christ's words about plucking out an offending right eye and arm.

However on returning home and looking up information about St. Virgil of Salzburg, I found that he did not exist till 710 A.D., well past the time of persecuting emperors. He was in fact a Scot, born in one of the Western Isles then named Heth. He was reared in the Christian faith as practised by St. Columba and the early Culdees. For some years he was abbot of Aghaboe, near Dublin. He had a great interest in geography, and perhaps for this reason decided to travel; he was known as the Geometer, measurer of the earth. He travelled as far as the court of Pepin, father of Charlemagne. In 745 Pepin – he was known as Pepin the Short – in spite of his small size conquered Duke Otto of Bavaria and compelled him to accept Virgil as bishop in his territories. This aroused the anger of St. Boniface, who preferred a bishop named John. It is amusing to read about his opinion of Bishop Virgil as a heretic who held unsuitable views about the earth as round, also for saying there were antipodes. The complaints were made to Rome, but no harm seems to have come to Bishop Virgil. He seems to have liked a joke; he pretended that he was a writer of cosmography named Aethicus Ister and that his inspiration came from St. Jerome!

However he administered his bishopric, as abbot of Sankt Peter, at first in the Irish way in which he had been brought up. 'At the wish of the people,' however, which probably means to avoid trouble, he agreed to be ordained after the Roman fashion on June 15th, 767. Shortly he converted the Alpine Slavs, who were fleeing from an invading race named the Avars. It was very much like the situation today.

On September 4th, 774, Virgil consecrated the new Cathedral of St. Rupert, Salzburg. Many centuries later, in 1181, his grave was found there. He was canonised by Pope Gregory IX on June 18th, 1233. As you know, his early theories about the shape of the earth have been accepted, although there are still a few people who believe that it is flat.

Part
Two

Names for Girls

Agnes (and Emerentiana)
Anne
Audrey (Etheldreda) and Hilda
Barbara
Bernadette
Bertha
Bridget
Catherine
Cecilia (and Agatha)
Clare
Dympna (and Tryphena)
Edith
Felicity (and Perpetua)
Frances
Geneviève, Jennifer, Ginevra
Helen, Helena
Hilda (with Audrey or
    Etheldreda)
Hildegard
Ida

Joan
Laura
Lucy
Madeleine, Magdalen
Marcella
Margaret
Martha
Matilda
Monica
Olga
Rose
Sarah
Sophia
Susanna, Susan
Teresa
Theodora (Dorothy)
Ursula
Veronica
Winifred
Zita

Agnes (and Emerentiana)

To understand the story of St. Agnes, it is necessary to know a little of what was being done to Christians by the early fourth century. The times were past when emperors could line the streets with tarred human torches to be set alight as they passed, or watch martyrs torn to pieces by wild beasts in the arenas of Rome and Carthage. The bravery with which these victims met their deaths not only aroused admiration for them, but curiosity about the faith which gave them courage. It therefore became the policy of the later emperors, who expected to be worshipped as gods themselves, to try to make Christians ridiculous.

A bishop was no longer burned alive, like St. Polycarp the aged martyr of Smyrna. On discovery and conviction, by now the bishop's right eye was burned out, and he was hamstrung, which means that the tendons behind both knees were cut through, making it impossible for him ever again to stand upright but to creep wherever he went, in mockery of the genuflection. Several of these one-eyed and crouching bishops were still alive by the time of the Council of Nicaea in 325, after the emperor Constantine had made Christianity the official religion. By then, Agnes was many years dead, having been martyred in 304 at the age of twelve.

The fate of women convicted of Christianity in her time was

perhaps even more horrible than that of the bishops. Their noses were cut off and they were placed in brothels, houses of prostitution. This was because it was known that Christians valued chastity. It also made it impossible for such women to escape without being recognised.

The emperor at that time was Diocletian, who liked to be called Jovius, head of the gods. Nevertheless it is thought that he himself would not have persecuted the Christians to quite the extent described, but that his subordinate, Galerius, forced him to do so. Galerius' fellow-general, or Caesar as both were called by then – the name had formerly only been the emperor's – was the father of Constantine, his first wife being Helena, who discovered the True Cross.

Meantime, it took great courage to be a Christian, even in secret. Agnes's family were rich Romans, and were Christian. It is possible that in youth they had met old men and women who remembered hearing, from their own elders, of the execution of a famous Roman citizen, St. Paul. Certainly his teachings, in particular the Letters to the Romans, would be familiar to Agnes from childhood. That her faith was strong enough for her to die at twelve years old, rather than renounce it, shows that it must have been taught to her from the beginning. Could you have done as much at that age, or could you now?

Agnes is generally shown with a lamb, which her name means. At twelve she was considered old enough to be married, and although her parents did not force her, a suitor was eager to have her as his wife. He does not sound a pleasant young man, and no doubt did not understand the general belief in those days, which St. Paul had himself held, that the world would soon come to an end and that it was better not to marry. The young man grew persistent, then spiteful when he met with no encouragement. He reported Agnes and her family to the authorities as Christians, and the girl's parents were obliged to confess their faith publicly. We do not know what happened to them, but Agnes was put in prison for further questioning, possibly because she was so young.

She must have kept silent, because they then dragged her before pagan idols, probably images of the emperor and his Caesars. The child refused to pay homage to them, and made the sign of the cross.

There was then only one fate for her. It is however known that her face was not mutilated; her head, severed from the body, was found long after. Meantime, all that seemed certain was that she had died.

Legends grew round the fact of her death, and among them one thing is clear: Agnes was not called upon to submit to rape. One version has it that she was removed bodily by heavenly means, another – this is probable – that she died at once. A third says her long hair protected her against assault from everyone except the persistent suitor, who was there; seeing her stripped naked, he was at once struck blind. Agnes forgave him and prayed for his sight to be restored, which happened; but she was then accused of being a sorceress, and condemned to be burned. However the flames were turned outwards to consume the watchers, sparing her. In the end she was beheaded by the sword, which last is certain: her head, that of a girl aged 12 years, was found and examined on 19th April, 1903. St. Pius X gave it to the church of St. Agnese in Agone, in the Piazza Navone in Rome.

St. Agnes is the patron of young girls. There is a town in Cornwall named after her, showing how far her devotion had spread. There are several paintings of her death, showing a bright light round her head and crowds about her. She is mentioned in the Canon of the Mass, in the writings of Ambrose and Prudentius, and the date of her death, 304 A.D. is only nine years before the official recognition of Christianity under Constantine. As for the emperor Diocletian, shortly after Agnes's death he suffered a mysterious depression, which forced him to abdicate and retire to his palace in Dalmatia. One wonders what he thought about in the eight years left to him. He died in 313, the very year of the Edict of Constantine, which ensured the free worship of Christ.

A young girl named Emerentiana is said to have been the foster-sister of St. Agnes, and was still a catechumen, which in those times meant that she had not yet been baptised; baptism was still a matter of total immersion and of course had to be arranged in secret. Whatever the mystery of Agnes' death, Emerentiana was found praying by her grave two days later. She was stoned to death either by official order, or by a hostile crowd. It was debated whether or not she had died a Christian; we ourselves would have no doubt, but in the end it was allowed that she had received the baptism of blood.

She is buried in the Via Nomentana in Rome, and her feast day is September 16th. She is also honoured on 30th June along with the other Roman martyrs. One of her relics is in the possession of Westminster Cathedral in London.

Anne

The name Anne, sometimes given as Anna or Hannah, occurs in the Old Testament as the name of Samuel's mother and, later, is known to have been that of the mother of Our Lady.

This is not recorded in the Bible, but in a very old book called the Protoevangelium Jacobi, written about 170 A.D. The writer's grandparents could have been alive in the time of Christ. You perhaps know how well your own grandparents recall names of people they knew or heard about when they were young.

This book was important enough at the time to be translated into eight languages – Greek, Latin, Syriac, Coptic, Armenian, Ethiopian, Georgian (in Russia) and Arabic. The whole

Christian world was thus made aware that Our Lady's parents were called Joachim and Anne.

In those times, the known world was small. By now, there is a shrine to St. Anne as far away as Canada. Originally the crusaders and, later, the Hansa merchants brought home news of the discoveries made in the Holy Land and on voyages; the merchant brotherhood travelled as far from home as Persia and India, bringing back jewels from Kashmir.

One of the Hanseatic towns the merchants built is Lübeck. It has changed very little from their time. Everywhere there are to be seen statues of St. Anne, also her figure painted on inn-signs and town houses. She is usually shown wearing green, with the Virgin in blue on her lap, and in the Virgin's lap a tiny Christ. A famous drawing exists by Leonardo da Vinci, who lived in the 16th century, showing St. Anne, the Virgin, and Christ as a little child. The three figures are grouped gracefully and the faces are very beautiful. This drawing, known as a cartoon – Leonardo meant to finish it as a painting, but he was a person who did a great many other things including a good try at designing aircraft – can be seen in the National Gallery in London, but copies are often available; you can probably even buy a postcard. The title is Leonardo's *Virgin and St. Anne*.

The story of St. Anne herself from the Protoevangelium says that her husband Joachim was a rich man respected in Israel. The couple lived, very probably, in a hill city named Sepphóris. Today its ruins, with great fallen marble pillars, are still to be seen in the hills just north of Nazareth. A painting hangs there in the open air, protected by the dry climate, of Joachim and Anne and their little child Mary crowned with flowers. Down the hill is a small ruined farm of the kind to which they may well have gone for goat's milk, cheese, and olives; there is still a grey stone wall to keep in goats, and a stunted olive orchard. Nobody lives there, or in the city, any more.

Joachim was reproached one day for having no children, and he felt the reproach so severely that he left his wife Anne and went off alone into the desert to fast and pray. After hearing nothing from him for some time, Anne thought he must be dead, and began to mourn because she was a widow, and childless. Then an angel appeared to her, and promised her she should bear a child who would do great things. It is rather like the story of Our Lady in the same situation, except that Anne already had a husband and believed herself barren.

At the same time, in the desert, Joachim had had the same vision as his wife. He hastened home, and messengers came to tell Anne her husband was returning. Full of joy, she hastened out to meet him at the city gate. They kissed, and this kiss between husband and wife, known as the Osculum, is said to be the only one portrayed in religious art which extols married life. Joachim and Anne are therefore particularly the saints of married couples. The Osculum was recorded by an artist who lived in the same century as Leonardo, but in a different country. He was a German named Albrecht Dürer. He is famous for his engravings, and the one described shows Joachim and Anne embracing at the gate while the neighbours look on, as neighbours do. This was a more important occasion than they knew: there was about to take place the Immaculate Conception of Our Lady. Some people still confuse this with the Virgin Birth, which was of course the birth of Christ to Mary herself by means of the Holy Spirit. The Immaculate Conception meant that two good and loving people conceived a child, probably late in life, in the same way as, for instance, John the Baptist was later conceived by ageing parents, or, much earlier, Samuel and Isaac to women thought barren.

Mary was born to the couple as promised, and unlike them had no original sin. We know this because she said so herself at Lourdes. Meantime her overjoyed mother Anne had, on hearing the angel's promise, vowed to dedicate her child to Temple service. This was in the same way as with the earlier Anna, whose son Samuel became a prophet.

Meantime, while Mary still lived as a little child in Sephóris, she must have been able to look out over the green-brown hills and deep valleys towards Nazareth. Perhaps she was even able to run down the hill to the farm. However when she was three years old, the records tell us, her parents took her, with two turtle doves as an offering, to the Temple, and she ran up the steps as though she was coming home; the story relates this. Presently she became a server in the Temple until the time of her betrothal to Joseph, probably when she was about fourteen years old.

Her mother Anne may meantime have been widowed; neither she nor Joachim had been young when their only child was born. She may have moved to Jerusalem to be near her daughter. A house still known as hers is to be seen beside the Pool of Siloam, where her grandson Jesus was to cause many to be cured by washing themselves in it. The house is not very grand, so perhaps after Joachim's death there was less money. St. Joseph after all, though a descendant of King David, was only a carpenter, perhaps also a bricklayer. The daughter of rich parents might well have been betrothed to somebody else. At that rate it is a good thing there was less money, as Joseph turned out to be exactly the right person.

Devotion to St. Anne grew quickly in the early Church, because it was realised, as somebody has written, that she is the point at which divinity enters into humanity. Later, when the angel came in turn to Mary herself, she remembered a prayer her mother must certainly have taught her and which Anne herself no doubt remembered when told to expect her own child. It is the earlier prayer of Anna, the mother of Samuel. Here it is in the translation by Bishop Challoner in the Douai version of the Bible.

My heart hath rejoiced in the Lord, and my horn is exalted in my God: my mouth is enlarged over my enemies: because I have joyed in thy salvation.

Anne

There is none holy as the Lord is; for there is none other beside thee, and there is none strong like our God.

Do not multiply to speak lofty things, boasting: let old matters depart from your mouth: for the Lord is a God of all knowledge, and to him are thoughts prepared.

The bow of the mighty is overcome, and the weak are girt with strength.

They that were full before have hired themselves out for bread: and the hungry are filled, so that the barren have borne many; and she that had many children is weakened.

The Lord killeth and maketh alive, he bringeth down to hell and bringeth back again.

The Lord maketh poor and maketh rich, he humbleth and he exalteth.

He raiseth up the needy from the dust, and lifteth up the poor from the dunghill: that he may sit with princes, and hold the throne of glory. For the poles of the earth are the Lord's, and upon them he hath set the world.

He will keep the feet of his saints, and the wicked shall be silent in darkness, because no man shall prevail by his own strength.

The adversaries of the Lord shall fear him: and upon them shall be thunder in the heavens. The Lord shall judge the ends of the earth, and he shall give empire to his king, and shall exalt the horn of his Christ.

That is in 1st Kings, chapter 2.* Compare it with the version you know of the Magnificat, and try to understand the old language. If you find it too difficult, there is a modern translation in your own Bible. Either way, you will agree that Mary almost certainly remembered the prayer she had learned from her mother Anne, who would know it from the old story of Anna, the mother of Samuel; a remarkable woman herself.

* Douai version.

Anne is the name the Queen chose for her daughter. It is also a special favourite for girls in Brittany. Not only is there a shrine there called St. Anne d'Auray which is famous, but the last duchess of Brittany was called Anne. She became queen of France, a fact which still angers many Bretons as it meant that their land was no longer separate. There is another famous shrine called St. Anne de Beaupré in Quebec. The feast day of Ss. Joachim and Anne is on July 26th; formerly hers was on 9th September. We should also remember the holy woman Anna in the Temple, a widow who with Simeon recognised the child Jesus when his parents brought him in, with two doves, for presentation to the priests. Anna was a prophetess and knew certain things in advance. She knew that this child would redeem Israel and would be, as Simeon had said, a light to lighten the Gentiles; but she also knew there would be sorrow. 'A sword shall pierce thy heart also,' she told Mary. This came true at the Crucifixion, when a lance pierced the heart of Christ.

Audrey (Etheldreda) and Hilda

Both these women were great saints, but while one who was active and well known in her lifetime is almost forgotten now, the other is remembered in ways she would not have expected!

St. Etheldreda's church in Ely Place, Holborn, is very famous and is one of the few which escaped damage during the Gordon Riots and earlier. Heads and figures of Elizabethan times can still be seen there, painted in colours as they would have been. However St. Etheldreda – the word 'ethel' means 'noble' – lived much earlier, in the days of the Saxon kings.

As a young widow, perhaps in her twenties, she was made to marry a little boy. He was Egfrid, king of Northumbria. When

Audrey (Etheldreda) and Hilda

Egfrid grew up he wanted a wife nearer his own age. Etheldreda's marriage to him was annulled, with her consent as she wanted to found a convent. Outside it, for many years, was held a fair. In early days, as now, cheap objects were sold there, and the word 'tawdry' began to be applied to them, as they were sold outside St. Audrey's; the name Etheldreda had been corrupted to this with the change in language from Saxon to Norman. St. Etheldreda herself would not have wanted to be regarded as cheap, but few now remember the allusion.

The other saint is Hild, or Hilda, of Whitby.

She was a princess of royal blood, born in 614. When she was 13 years old she was baptised, and went to Paris to a convent where her sister Hereswitha, also to become a saint, was a nun. Hilda stayed there for some years, and her piety and wisdom became so widely spoken of that St. Aidan, the bishop of Lindisfarne, or perhaps Finan his successor, sent for Hild to become abbess of the convent at Hartlepool.

After some time there she went to the place with which her name will always be associated; Whitby, on the north-east coast of Yorkshire, 300 feet above the sea. There she became abbess of a monastery for women and for men. The women took precedence. There is a great deal of argument nowadays about this kind of thing, but Abbess Hild was no violent feminist; she treated everyone alike, wisely and tactfully, never domineering. Bishops and kings used to visit her for her advice.

The Synod of Whitby was held in her time in 644. It decided such factors as the primacy of Rome and the placing of the tonsure, because at that time certain of the Celtic monks shaved their foreheads instead of, as now, the crown of the head. There were other important decisions.

Hild died in the year 680. A nun 13 miles away saw her soul carried up to heaven by angels. She is an example of what women can achieve by quietly using the gifts they were given, not trying to demand those of others as a right. There is a proper way to do everything.

Barbara

The legend of St. Barbara contains more truth than is evident on the surface. At first it seems like one more fairy story of a princess imprisoned in a tower.

Nevertheless although Barbara was a very early saint, miracles were ascribed to her soon after her death, and belief in her remained strong through the Middle Ages and into the late fifteenth century. There is a famous painting of Edward IV's sister Margaret, who married Charles the Bold of Burgundy about 1470, painted as St. Barbara in Flanders. There is also Santa Barbara in Argentina, Brazil, Mexico and California.

The original story is that Barbara's father, whose name was Dioscaurus, shut his daughter up in a tower because she was so beautiful. This seems an odd reason until one looks further. A beautiful daughter was an asset in marriage, and could make her father powerful if, for instance, she married a prince or chieftain. We are told that Barbara had already refused offers of marriage from several princes, and it is probable that she had taken a vow of chastity. This meant that she was a Christian, but had not told her father, who does not sound as if he had an understanding of such things. It was completely foreign to the pagan beliefs that a young woman should not marry provided she was healthy.

The tower in which Dioscaurus imprisoned his daughter was, we are told, full of idols. It is probable that these were fertility images, and that Dioscaurus was trying to accustom his daughter to the idea of marriage by forcing her to look at them constantly. However they say not even prison walls can keep Christ out, and as Barbara had not been baptised she persuaded a workman to make a window in her tower and arranged to be baptised through it. She then smashed and disfigured the idols left by her father, who was away.

When Dioscaurus returned he was furious, and threatened his daughter with a sword. Some versions say that he cut off her head, but that it was miraculously restored to her neck. However, he then had Barbara beaten and tortured. She was already consoled by a vision of Our Lord, which sustained her through anything that might happen.

Finally her father killed her, and the story says he was promptly consumed by fire: doubtless this happened later if not sooner. Miracles began to occur in the town soon after Barbara's death, and devotion to her memory grew steadily and spread through Europe. Her story resembles, in many details, that of other young woman saints of the early period; their common factor is the preservation of their chastity following a vow. The tale of a wicked father occurs also in the story of St. Dympna, and the tower itself may be as old as the ancient Greek legend of Danäe, whose father shut her up in one. It is worth remembering the words of St. Paul, in the old version I like best; *For I am persuaded that neither death, nor life, nor angels, nor principalities, nor powers, nor things present, nor things to come, nor height, nor depth, nor any other creature, shall be able to separate us from the love of God, which is in Christ Jesus our Lord.*

G.K. Chesterton wrote a long poem called *The Legend of St. Barbara.* Try to obtain it from the library, as it is out of print.

Bernadette

Lourdes is a place from which can be seen the fantastic shapes of the Pyrenees, between France and Spain. I always think God must have taken a pair of scissors and snipped out whatever shapes occurred to him.

In a low valley nearby, with the river Garve running through below the town, a family named Soubirous lived. They were very poor, but loving and devout: it was said that an angry word was never heard in their house. Their eldest child, Marie-Bernarde, always called Bernadette, was delicate; she had asthma, and the attacks often kept her away from school. She fell behind the other pupils and was considered stupid. However she was not stupid, merely gentle and obedient, and she had courage to stand up for what she knew to be the truth.

Bernadette was a great help at home, and one day as usual – it was Thursday, 11th February, 1868, when she was almost sixteen – she went down to where there was a cave near the river where pigs sheltered, to gather firewood.

It was the last place where anything miraculous could be expected to happen, and Bernadette was expecting nothing of the kind. When a most beautiful lady, in a white robe and blue sash, with golden roses on her feet, appeared on a ledge of rock just inside the upper part of the cave, the young girl knelt. She did not know who the lady was, and in later attempts to describe her said that sculptors who tried to make images from her own descriptions had come nowhere near expressing the lady's beauty. Her visions – by then there had been several – could not fully be described.

However by then she knew who the lady was, as she had asked her and had been told 'I am the Immaculate Conception.' It was said, in the dialect Bernadette knew; *Que soy era Immaculada Councepciou.* She could not possibly have heard of the doctrine, which was not then generally taught or known about. It was partly this that convinced the Church authorities, who at first would not believe Bernadette, that she had truly seen the Mother of God.

Secondly, the lady told Bernadette to go and wash at the spring where watercress grew. There was no sign of a spring there, and by then the news of Bernadette's visions had spread, and crowds came to watch her. She dug with her hands at the spot she had been told of, but merely smeared her face with earth. The crowd turned away, shrugging their shoulders; that Soubirous girl had never been strong in her wits.

That same evening, a man was passing the spot. He saw water gushing up from the ground. Since then, this has become the famous healing source at Lourdes. It has now been channelled into a bath to which, all the year round, sick people come. Some are cured, others not, but all come away with an acceptance of their state they did not have before. Voluntary helpers, many of them young people, help to push the invalid chairs and stretchers to and from the baths. Above on the hill is the church Our Lady told Bernadette to have built. The space outside the grotto is packed at all times and seasons by pilgrims and priests; Mass is said in the grotto itself, often to huge crowds, but the best time to come is very early in the morning, before anyone else is about, and to see the statue made from Bernadette's description on the ledge of rock where the visions appeared.

Bernadette herself entered the convent at Nevers, some distance off, at the age of twenty. She died only a few years later, still young. Her incorrupt body can still be seen there; the face is very beautiful. It has become fashionable in Lourdes to call oneself Soubirous, whether one is entitled to the name or not!

St. Bernadette was canonised in 1933. Her feast day is April 16th.

Bertha

Every schoolchild is, or used to be, taught about Bertha, the Frankish princess who married King Ethelbert of Kent and persuaded him to allow St. Augustine to bring Christianity to England in 597. However the schoolchildren are not normally taught that there were two Berthas, about whom there persists great confusion.

Both were Franks, and both were daughters of the Meroving dynasty of *rois fainéants*, phantom kings descended from Clovis, the first Christian ruler. However one Bertha had a father named Charibert and the other a father named Haribert. The first lived in the eighth century and married Pepin the Short, becoming the mother of Charlemagne. She was known as *Berthe au grand pied*, Bertha with the big foot, as she had one foot bigger than the other. Her son Charlemagne was an enormous person, so presumably both his feet were large.

To return to the sixth century and our Bertha, she came to England as a bride accompanied by Lindhard, bishop of Senlis. At that time the court was pagan, but they must have received the bishop with courtesy. King Ethelbert was an intelligent man who was the first ruler to have laws put in written form. He seems to have listened to his wife's counsels with regard to the promised missionaries offered by the Pope, St. Gregory the Great. You probably know the story of how he had seen fair-haired little boys for sale in the Roman slave market, asked what nation they belonged to, and on being told they were Angles, said '*Non Angli, sed angeli,*' and arranged for the country's conversion. He was one of our greatest Popes.

It must have been a strange and memorable moment when Queen Bertha and King Ethelbert received the party of forty-one black-clad monks on the Isle of Thanet, led by Augustine bearing the Host and, nearby, the square white banner of the Vernacle, the Sacred Face, blessed by Pope Gregory, who would have liked to come himself. A residence – it would be made of wood – had been prepared for the missionaries at Canterbury, and soon the king, no doubt also prepared by Bertha and Lindhard, agreed to be baptised. As still happens, everybody who was anybody followed suit. It is said that Augustine baptised 10,000 converts in one day in the river Swale. However they were not forced at the sword's point, as happened presently in Russia. In fact, many returned to pagan worship later, including Ethelbert's and Bertha's sons. Nevertheless it was a beginning.

Ethelbert and his queen are shown in a mosaic in St. Gregory's Chapel in Westminster Cathedral, London, but unfairly only Ethelbert is given a halo.

Queen Bertha – in those times the word queen merely meant king's companion – died before 616, which is the year her husband died. There are numerous legends about her, always confusing her with Bertha of the Big Foot, who was not yet born.

Bridget

Bridget, or Bride, was a child of great sanctity, so much so that St. Patrick loved her as a daughter and when he was dying, asked that when Bride should die her remains might be placed beside his. This request was not carried out by his followers.

Her story is so old that it is taken for granted, and in Ireland Bridget is still a favourite name. Few now know that she founded the first religious house for women at Kildare. Many miracles are attributed to her. She died aged 73. Her feast is on 1st February.

Irish missionaries went to Austria and Germany, and it is probable that their influence spread to Sweden, which remained a heathen country for much longer. By the 12th century, however, St. Bridget of Sweden was able to found an order named after her and which in turn spread to England, the Brigittines of Syon. I found a postcard of her carved head in Stockholm in a church there, where not many saints are to be found portrayed. She wore a caul, a netted headdress and was shown as a young woman. Like St. Catherine of Siena, she encouraged the end of the great schism which took the popes to Avignon and even raised antipopes. She was canonised in 1391, only 18 years after her death, and the house at Syon was built in her memory by our Henry V, the victor of Agincourt, who for once took leisure from his French wars.

Catherine

There are at least three saints of this name who are well worth knowing about, and only a little can be said here.

The earliest was Catherine of Alexandria. She was of royal blood and, like many such ladies of the time, very well educated and learned. We do not know how she came to believe in the Christian faith, which at that time was still persecuted.

Shortly after she was baptised, Catherine had a vision of the Christ Child, who put a wedding ring on her finger. This is known as the Mystical Marriage. News of such matters reached the emperor, and he assembled 90 pagan philosophers, all of them learned men, to try to confound Catherine in public. They not only failed to manage it, but she converted them and, also, the empress. For this last, Catherine was condemned to be broken on a wheel. However this attempt of the emperor's failed also, as the wheel flew into pieces and its spokes injured bystanders. He then made sure that Catherine would die by having her beheaded.

Her feast day is November 25th. She is generally shown with a crown to show her royal blood, a book to show her learning, and the wheel.

Catherine of Siena was born about 1347. She was a twin, and the 23rd child of a dyer. She was therefore looked down on by the grand people of the town, who treated everything she said and did as presumption. Nevertheless Catherine always knew what she was talking about and, like Christ, spoke with authority. She cut off her hair at an early age, and was associated with the Dominicans in her anxiety for a crusade against the Turks. In 1368 she had a vision; shortly, for she may not have been able to read or write, she dictated letters to companions who acted as her secretaries. At that time there was the great schism, which led to antipopes living in Avignon. This situation caused Catherine great distress, and she used all her growing influence to try to put an end to the divisions and to restore a single Pope in Rome. Her *Dialogue* is among the most famous of her writings. There is a portrait of her painted during her lifetime, which shows a slim handsome woman in a white veil, holding a lily.

Catherine suffered such anguish over the schism that she took a seizure. She also received the stigmata, as St. Francis had done, but no one could see the marks except herself. She died in 1380, and many years afterwards her body was incorrupt. Her head is preserved in the church of San Damiano, Siena, the place where there was so much unkind gossip about her.

St. Catherine of Genoa is less well known than the above two, except in her native town. She was married to a man named Giuliano Adorno, and at first he caused her much unhappiness by his dissolute way of living. About this time Catherine had a vision of Christ on the cross, and she kept praying for her husband. Giuliano went bankrupt, and this made him change his ways. He became a Franciscan tertiary and together, they ran the hospital at Pammatone without payment.

All these were great women, and there are many others of the name who have been canonised for different reasons; for instance St. Catherine Labouré, of the Miraculous Medal. St. Catherine of Siena, the dyer's daughter described above, is however one of the Fourteen Holy Helpers and was named patron of Italy, together with St. Francis, by Pius XII.

Cecilia and Agatha

I have included these two saints together to show the contrast in their lives; the first had an understanding lover, the second a suitor who did not understand. In both cases the chief love of the young women was for Christ, for whom they died.

St. Cecilia is usually shown playing an organ and is even said, wrongly, to have invented it. As she lived either in 229 or 180, and as the organ of Winchester Cathedral was considered an unknown marvel when it was installed in the twelfth century, this is one more attempt to fill the gap that exists about many early saints and to make one different from the next. In the case of Cecilia the result has been so many conflicting stories that they may well refer to more than one person.

One source says Cecilia was blind. This is unlikely, as her parents gave her in marriage, but if she was so it may account for the fact that she is said to have been musical; a blind girl of good family would be taught to play some instrument to pass the time. However Cecilia spent much of her time in prayer, and also wore penitential clothing under her robe. As many Christian young women then did, she had taken a vow of chastity.

It must be remembered that at that early time there were no convents or monasteries to enter. A life of chastity had to be lived in a hostile world. St. Paul's teachings led many men and women to avoid marriage, as it was thought the end of the world was near, also Christ himself had said that in the next, there would be no marrying or giving in marriage.

Nevertheless Cecilia's parents were determined that she should marry a young pagan, Valerian. Fortunately he loved Cecilia, and after their wedding found her at prayer with, so the story puts it, an angel with wings of flame standing between them. This may merely mean that Valerian had enough courtesy to know that he must not touch his wife without her leave. In fact he respected her beliefs so much that he himself became a Christian very shortly, also his brother Tiburtius. Both young men became deacons, and the household continued in this way undisturbed for four years. Then Cecilia and her husband and his brother were denounced to the authorities.

There is conflicting evidence about what happened next. Some say Cecilia was beheaded, but that three strokes failed to kill her and at the sight of her courage, the executioner became a Christian. Another version says she was suffocated in a hot bath (this certainly happened to the second wife of Constantine) and gave her house to become a church; it is still said to be the foundations of one in Rome.

The third version is one I have never read, but only remember what I saw. Many years ago I visited the catacombs, and among the dark tortuous passages where the earliest Christian meetings were held, came on a recumbent marble statue of a beautiful young girl. She was portrayed lying exactly as they had found her, incorrupt, in the seventeenth century; a sculptor had carved the body exactly as it was. She was smaller than we are today, possibly just over five feet tall. There was a stab-wound in her throat at the left side. Her right hand had the fingers twisted in the sign of the Trinity. The sight of this little figure was immensely touching, and I was told that the body had been that of St. Cecilia. This may have been mistaken, but whoever she was had died clinging hard to her belief.

St. Cecilia may or may not have been blind, but she is the patron of the blind as well as of music. The latter seems to have happened by accident, though of course some say she heard the singing of her angel. In fact, about the time the girl's body was found in the catacombs, there was a concert in London. It happened to be St. Cecilia's day, November 22nd, and so she was adopted! Blow, Purcell, Dryden, Clarke and Handel all subscribed to the legend, and since then there has been a St. Cecilia's Day concert yearly.

St. Agatha's story is sadder than Cecilia's; she had no Valerian to sustain her. Agatha was a Sicilian girl with most beautiful breasts, and seeing her the consul desired to marry her. He could not understand the vow of chastity she had taken, and being an arrogant man ordered her arrest. This meant not only prison, but a brothel. Agatha resisted attempts to violate her, and the vengeful consul ordered her to be stretched on a rack and tortured dreadfully by red-hot rods, crushing and mutilation. After these first tortures Agatha had a vision of St. Peter, who healed her ruined breasts; but on the renewal of torture she died.

She is invoked by women suffering from diseases of the breast, such as cancer; and is prayed to by the inhabitants below Mount Etna, as she is supposed to be able to stop the flow of lava when the volcano erupts. St. Lucy, who lived later in Sicily, had a vision of St. Agatha during her own torments, which helped her, in her turn, to die as bravely.

Clare

You have chosen the patron saint of television!

She is also the saint of good weather. These are the things least well known about her, but they arose from the fact that her name means 'clear light.'

Before her birth, her mother Ortolana di Favarone was praying in church at Assisi. The year was 1193. Somewhere outside in the town a boy of eleven, Francesco Bernardone, may have been playing in the streets with his friends or learning Latin with his tutor. He knew nothing yet of experiences such as the one which came to Ortolana as she prayed. She was in fact a little afraid, for this was her first child and she asked for a safe delivery. She heard a voice say in answer 'Do not fear, for you will bring forth with joy a clear light which will illumine the world.' When the baby girl was born she was therefore christened Chiara, in English Clare.

Clare di Favarone grew up to be not only beautiful, but a very good child who prayed often. She was obedient and generous, which last was easy as her parents were rich as well as noble. The Bernardone family were perhaps as rich, and Francesco's mother came of a distinguished family in Picardy; but her husband was a merchant, although a very successful one. Clare's parents expected her to marry suitably to her rank; they were not alarmed over the fact that she gave alms to the poor; it was the usual behaviour of a noblewoman.

However by the time Clare was eighteen years old she had already met Francesco Bernardone, and the town had by then decided that he was mad. Five years previously he had disppointed all his father's hopes for him, had renounced all possessions and had embraced poverty in order to imitate Christ in the Gospels. Francis, as we call him, and Clare were deeply attracted to one another, and had they met in any other circumstances would almost certainly have married and lived happily ever after. However to love somebody is to understand him, and Clare loved Francis enough to want to abandon her life of comfort and ease and follow his teachings. She asked him to advise her as to what to do. As a result, she left her family, her mother and sisters, took off her rich clothes and jewels and cut off her beautiful long hair, accepting instead the plain habit of a Franciscan. She consecrated herself to follow Francis, not in person for he would not permit this, but in spirit, perhaps enabling other women to do the same. Christ in the Gospels had been followed by women; she, Clare, would found her own order based on the rule of Francis.

She continued to receive his advice and help as long as he lived. For a time he put her in various convents, then finally established her and her followers in San Damiano, one of the churches he had rebuilt. Clare was to remain there for 42 years in poverty and seclusion, practising the rule with her nuns, who became known as the Poor Clares.

There are two stories which show that Clare was not always within convent walls. One day she was on a journey and met Francis on the road, walking the same way. He did not think it proper that they should walk together and suggested that they take separate paths, but Clare said 'If you see the roses bloom now when it is winter, you will know God sees fit for us to walk in one another's company.' The wintry stems burst into flower, and the two friends walked and talked together till the journey's end with great joy. On another occasion, some years after, they met again by arrangement in the church, and it was said a shining and marvellous light was seen from within the building while these two holy persons talked together once again.

Otherwise, it was a life of simplicity and contemplation, poverty and, often, hunger. Francis and his friars used to have begging bowls for food as they went about the public ways to preach, but the Poor Clares, unable to leave their convent, had to rely on scraps placed in charity outside the gate. When there was no food left and they were starving, they used to ring a bell in the hope that some would be brought. This practice was still the case in Ireland in the last century and may be so in places today.

The conditions in which Poor Clares live are harsh, almost unchanged from Clare's own day. The stone floors are cold against their sandalled feet, and they sleep on hard pallets and know nothing of luxury. However anyone who has seen a Poor Clare, face to face, knows that she is happy. To have shed all possessions, as Christ himself did and as Francis tried to do, means that certain things are gained which cannot even be imagined by those who cling to belongings, money and importance. Not all of us have the strength to do this or are called to; most of us are like the young man in the Bible who turned away because he was rich.

Clare had not chosen an easy life in any way, even in the founding of her Order. The Church authorities thought that she ought to follow the Benedictine model, and this was not what she knew Francis had intended for her. She fought the decision partly alone, as at the beginning she was for some time without the counsels of Francis, who was absent on his voyages to the East. However Clare at last had support from her family, who not only forgave her for leaving them but finally joined her in the convent. A few years after Clare had taken the habit in 1212, her sister Agnes entered San Damiano. Ortolana herself, perhaps remembering the time before Clare's birth, followed not long after, then a second sister, Beatrice. By 1216, Pope Innocent III had allowed the vow of poverty, a new thing then. Clare had won her fight, but she was already ill. From 1224, knowing by then that Francis was blind and had not long to live, until her own death long after in 1253, Clare of Assisi was almost constantly on a sickbed. The death of Francis in 1226 finished a part of her life. He would not allow her to be with him as he was dying, beyond the thickness of a single wall; but he gave her permission to look on his face when he was dead. She had 27 years still to live.

She had the consolation of a great devotion to the Mystical Body of Christ in the Eucharist. This devotion, and her prayers, together with those of her nuns, are supposed to have saved Assisi from the Saracens in 1240 and the year following.

When she died – there is a painting, made much later by an Austrian, of her deathbed, with women saints in rich robes and haloes at the far side, her mourning nuns in plain habits at the near side, and above a vision of Christ with her soul on his arm – Clare was buried first in San Giorgio, where Francis' body by then was. Later on her own body, found to be incorrupt, was transferred to the new church of Santa Chiara in Assisi, where it still lies. St. Clare had been canonised five years previously, in 1255.

There are two other feasts connected with her besides the day of her death, 23rd September; there is also the *inventio* and the *translatio* of the body as already described. Images of St. Clare

are shown with the Rule, a lily, a crucifix, or a ciborium or monstrance in token of her particular devotion. As said, she is invoked for television and the weather, also childbirth and in cases of eye disease, remembering her name 'clear light'.

Dympna and Tryphena

Both of these stories are worse than anything on television, so if you dislike horrors do not read them. They are both from very early times when the world was largely pagan.

Dympna, or Dymphna, was an Irish princess or possibly a Breton one. Both countries had several kings at that time, and both had a common language. The Celtic race had fled out of the parts of Britain invaded by the Saxons, and had inhabited Wales with its mountains, remote Cornwall, Ireland and Brittany. To this day Welshmen and Bretons can understand one another's language.

Tryphena was certainly a Breton princess. Both she and Dympna were very beautiful, devoutly Christian, and were betrayed by the very men who ought to have been their protectors; in one case the father, in the other the husband.

Dympna's father was one of the lesser kings of Ireland or of Armorica, which is the ancient name for Brittany. He had a lovely wife who died when their daughter was fourteen. The broken-hearted king said he would not marry again until a woman as beautiful as his dead wife could be found. He sent ambassadors to all lands, but they only returned with the same message; nowhere in the world was there anyone as beautiful as the princess Dympna. The king then determined to marry his own daughter.

This would have been a state of affairs known as incest, which from earliest times has been a crime regarded with horror. You may know the story of the Greek king Oedipus, who discovered that he had married his own mother, and blinded himself to propitiate the gods. The only known acceptance of incest, apart from the gods themselves, was among the Pharaohs of Egypt, who regarded themselves as a sacred race who must keep the blood in the family. Akhenaton, an early Pharaoh, had only daughters by his wife Nefertiti, and tried to have a son by one of them; but the child was only another girl, who died. After Akhenaton's death the princess in question was married to Tutankhamun, of whom you have heard, and he also was a very close relation; but he died young and the couple had no children.

Later, with Christianity, the Popes made rules against the marriage of closely related persons. Consanguinity within the forbidden degrees prevented marriage in Christian countries. No Pope would ever have permitted the marriage of Dympna to her father.

She fled across seas to Geele, in the Low Countries, and is said to have become a hermit there. However she was not given much time, as her father found out where she had gone and at once pursued her. Still Dympna refused to agree, and in rage he cut off her head with his sword.

Dympna's remains were found and identified at Geele in the 13th century. As they were on the point of building an asylum for the insane there and needed a patron saint, Dympna was chosen and is still the patroness of the mentally afflicted.

Tryphena's story is less well documented and reminds one of the tale of Bluebeard. This time the story is certainly Breton. At that early time the land had several chiefs who called themselves kings, and one king was named, unsuitably, Conamor. Conamor used to eat his wives as they were on the point of giving birth to his children. This is slightly nastier than the habits of the god Saturn, who only ate the children as they were born. Perhaps Conamor was trying to go one better. At any rate, after the most recent wife had been devoured, he caught sight of a Christian princess named Tryphena, who as already stated was very beautiful, and fell in love with her. He asked her father, a neighbouring king, for her hand. This king was a Christian like his daughter, and understandably neither he nor she were enthusiastic about the offer. However both considered it their duty to have Conamor baptised if possible, and he promised that this should happen if he was allowed to marry Tryphena. He also promised not to eat her. She was moreover to be allowed to return to her father if she ever felt the need.

Under the circumstances, Tryphena felt that it was her duty to become the wife of Conamor. They were married with great rejoicings and the blessing of the Church, and the celebrations continued for a long time and everyone seemed happy. However as the months passed Tryphena knew that she was expecting a child, and the more attentive Conamor became, the more worried she did, as this was the stage at which he had eaten all his former wives. In the end Tryphena was so frightened she escaped one night and tried to return to her father. Perhaps it would have been better to have stayed, as Conamor, feeling that he had been betrayed by her, followed her into the forest, caught up with her and slew her with his sword. At least he did not eat her, which means that he kept part of the bargain.

Next morning, poor Tryphena's father found her body, and beside it a baby son who had been born alive from it. He took the baby to the abbot Gildas, later a famous Breton saint, to be brought up, and in the end the boy became a monk in the abbey. No one knows what became of Conamor or if he returned to eating more wives.

Remember that both these stories are very old, and that the times were brutal. Both of these beautiful young women are remembered as martyrs for Christ.

Edith

Edith is a pretty name to choose for confirmation, and there is certainly a saint of that name; she died when she was 13. She was a royal Saxon princess, the daughter of Edgar the Peaceful. She was taken into Wilton convent as a little child and lived there all her short life. She became much loved by the nuns and also the poor, to whom she was always generous. This is really all that is known about her except that, when they offered to make her abbess, she refused, and died shortly after. 'She never left the world, she never knew it,' they said of her.

Many things are lost and forgotten from early England, but the convent at Wilton was always known as St. Edith's Convent. It became the practice to send royal maidens there for their education, while awaiting marriage or, like Edith, hoping to become nuns. One who did not want to be a nun was a later Edith, who used to jump on her veil! She was a Scots princess who married Henry I of England, youngest son of William the Conqueror. She changed her name to Matilda in honour of her husband's mother and also, because he told her the English would not be able to pronounce the name Edith, which is odd, as Edward the Confessor's queen was another Edith who was well remembered. There is one place in England called Edith Weston, which was her land. See if you can discover a second, and also if you can find out how the Anglo-Saxons spelt the name of Edith.

Felicity and Perpetua

Among the wonderful sixth-century mosaics at Ravenna in Italy, there is a panel in the archbishop's chapel showing the heads of two young women, one placed above the other. It is dated four centuries after they died; they were among the earliest Christian martyrs, in 202 A.D.

It can be seen at once, looking at the mosaic, that their stations in life were quite different. The upper head wears a richly jewelled cap and an ornate necklace over a banded robe. The lower head is that of a plainly dressed servant.

She was in fact a slave. Her name was Felicitas, or Felicity in the modern version. Her mistress was called, in full, Vibia Perpetua. Both young women were Carthaginians.

Slaves like Felicity often had an extremely hard life, in particular if they belonged to an unkind master or mistress. They had no rights as we know them, being the absolute property of their owners. However a clever or learned slave was regarded as of great value. In fact Perpetua and Felicity were not only mistress and slave, but friends. It is even possible that it was through the humble Felicity that Perpetua came into contact with the Christian faith. However it happened, both were at one in their belief and prepared to give their lives for it. To be a Christian at that time was extremely dangerous. There had already been dreadful persecutions under earlier Roman emperors; Carthage by then belonged to Rome. Perpetua's father was a senator. Who her husband was we do not know, and in the events that follow he is not named at all. Almost certainly he was not in sympathy with the new faith. Perpetua had recently borne him a child, and was still nursing it. Felicity was expecting one. It is possible that the master of the house, owner of his slaves, was the father of both children. In these days that would make for jealousy and not friendship, but mistress and maid remained devoted and, in that year of their martyrdom, were taking instruction together from Saturus, a cathechist, and had met other Christians secretly in Carthage. This was a hundred and fifty years before St. Augustine taught there and even the first known hermit, St. Anthony of Egypt, may only just have been born. There were however examples to remember; Justin Martyr had vainly tried to persuade an earlier emperor of the perfection of the Christian faith, and only forty-six years before Felicity's time, in Smyrna, the aged bishop Polycarp had preferred to be burned to death rather than curse the name of Christ. That last was a test applied to all suspected Christians. 'Ninety-six years have I known him, and he has never done me any harm; why then should I curse his name?' the old bishop replied. The story of his brave death must have given courage to the two young women so soon to die themselves.

Carthage was in North Africa, near present-day Tunis. It had once been a powerful city by reason of its harbours, which allowed its merchants, the Phoenicians, to trade by sea with far countries. The rising state of Rome lacked any port, and made this an excuse to wage war with Carthage; there were three of these, known as the Punic Wars. In the end Rome won, despite the brilliant Carthaginian general Hannibal, who as you have probably heard took an army across the Alps using elephants for transport. That had been long before the time of Felicity and Perpetua, and by their day Carthage was a mere Roman province, though an important one. It still kept its forum, where senators such as Perpetua's father spoke and helped to govern under the orders of Rome.

The Roman emperor at that time was in fact an African, Septimius Severus. He travelled a great deal and later visited Britain, as the Phoenicians and Julius Caesar had done. Meantime, having spent two years in nearby Egypt, he paid a visit to Carthage on his way back to Rome. There he intended giving magnificent celebrations to mark the marriage of his son.

Perhaps as a rehearsal, or perhaps to please the Carthaginians, he ordered a series of entertainments there also. Among other attractions there would be wild-beast shows in the arena. It was a fashionable amusement already in Rome to watch Christians being torn to pieces by lions, panthers and leopards, although the crowds could not understand their bravery in face of death. Another cruel sport was to watch gladiators fight one another until one or the other was killed and the victor, waving his short sword, would be loudly cheered and expected to come back to fight again. A gladiator who survived many fights could become famous and could make a great deal of money. It is rather like our boxing matches and, lately, Wimbledon.

Emperor Septimius Severus needed victims for the wild-beast shows, and he therefore ordered a rounding up of anyone suspected of attending the Christian love-feasts. Among those arrested, though they had not yet been baptised, were Felicity and her mistress Perpetua, also four men whose names we know, including Saturus the catechist.

The arrest of Perpetua created great scandal in the city, as her family was important. Her father the senator, whose favourite child she was – there had been a little boy, Dinocrates, who had died of cancer – begged his daughter to recant. Although Perpetua was anxious about her baby, whom she could no longer feed – her milk had dried up on arrest, which is not a miracle as was thought then, but a known happening in cases of shock – she refused. The baby had meantime been given into the care of others. For a time Perpetua was deprived also of the comfort of her friend, as Felicity, being pregnant, was not allowed by Roman law to be put to death. However she gave birth to her child, a daughter, prematurely and was at once put in prison with the rest.

Felicity and Perpetua were then baptised together, which meant that they could share in the full rites of the Church. Again, this time in the public forum, her father tried to persuade his daughter – she was only twenty-two – to save her life. Again

Felicity and Perpetua

Perpetua refused. She had been strengthened by a vision while she slept. She had seen a golden ladder, with between it and herself swords and dragons. Perpetua stepped over the dragons and ignored the swords. She then climbed the ladder, and at the top was a meadow, where many persons waited in white robes. In the centre was a tall man with white hair, clad as a shepherd 'whose feet we saw not'. He said 'Welcome, child,' and fed her a white curdlike substance which tasted sweet when she awoke from the vision. She had also received the assurance that her little brother Dinocrates was in heaven with the rest.

She managed to write all of this down in the first three chapters of a book called the *Passio Perpetuae et Felicitatis*. It was completed by Saturus. It bears many likenesses to the Book of Revelation, but this would have been unknown to the writers at that time. The account itself must have been written in great haste. After only three days Perpetua, Felicity and the rest were flogged, given a blow each on the face, and led out to the arena and the waiting crowds. One account says they were then beheaded, but there is more detail given in another which is more likely given the conditions then. Felicity – and it must be remembered that she had just given birth to a child and had then been flogged – was bitten in the head by a leopard who ran with the other animals into the arena, having purposely been kept without food for some days. Seeing her maid's distress, Perpetua came over to comfort her. It is probable that Felicity died soon. Perpetua herself, being a woman of rank, attracted more attention and, by then, admiration from the bloodthirsty crowd. She had entered the arena 'abashing with the high spirit in her eyes the gaze of all' and singing a psalm. The Christians had earlier made a love-feast of the free meal offered to those about to die, and had given each other the kiss of peace. Perpetua had then refused to put on the mocking dress of a priestess of Ceres, pagan goddess of harvest; having received with the rest lashes and the blow on the face, she fought with an Egyptian gladiator and overcame him. There was then brought in a savage cow for her to fight. She conquered this animal also, having no remembrance afterwards of the fight or knowledge of her wounds, which had to be shown to her.

Her long hair was by then dishevelled, and she pinned it up lest she be thought to be mourning (the same thing was done, sixteen centuries later, by St. Margaret Clitherow on the way to her own terrible death) and presently a second gladiator was brought to fight Perpetua, and at the first attempt was still unsuccessful. The crowds were howling in excitement and admiration, and to finish the business the authorities ordered the man to kill her. Perpetua guided his hand to her throat. 'Perhaps so great a woman would not have been slain unless she willed it,' they wrote of her.

For a long time the story of the death of Perpetua was read out at church services as an inspiration. We hear less about Felicity; but there must be a reason why her name is frequently put before that of her mistress. Perhaps it is only because both friends would have understood that the first shall be last and the last first; or it is possible, as already stated, that it was the young slave herself who brought her mistress to the knowledge of Christ. The news often spread, as it had done at the beginning, from lowly places.

The two friends were buried together, and their tomb was identified in the ruins of Carthage as late as 1907. A relic of St. Perpetua is in the crypt of Westminster Cathedral. The feast day of the two saints is on March 6th.

Frances

St. Frances of Rome, Santa Francesca Romana, was born in 1384. She desired to become a nun, but was forced by her family to marry at the age of 13. Fortunately the bridegroom, a young man named Lorenzo Ponziani, loved her. He made her a considerate husband and their married life lasted forty years. It is said that Frances was the perfect type of Christian wife, but this is stated to be because she devoted herself to the poor, and also founded a convent for Oblates. One feels a little sorry for Lorenzo.

Political and other troubles meant that at one time Frances had to hand over their young son to the authorities. She was also compelled to travel a great deal, back and forth. Her unending penances lessened her attraction for her husband, who after his initial support lost patience for a time, being only human. The truth is that it is as great a mistake to force a marriage as to force anyone to take conventual vows; both states should be entered into with full consent. However Lorenzo regained his affection for his wife before he died in 1436.

Frances immediately entered her convent, and spent the rest of her life – not very long – in penance and prayer. She died in 1440. It was 1608 before she was canonised, but she has always been a favourite with the Romans, and has lately replaced St. Christopher as the official patron of travellers, having had much experience.

Geneviève, Jennifer, Ginevra

Jennifer, Ginevra, Geneviève, are all the same name; that of a wonderful woman who lived in Paris in the fifth century, long before it became the capital of France.

Her story would be astonishing if only because of the length of her life. At a time when most people considered themselves lucky to live to be 50, St. Genevieve survived to be 92! She was born in 420 and died in 512, after having achieved more things by prayer than others did with armies.

She took the veil at the age of 15. It was an age when, although the Roman empire was crumbling, it was still regarded as the central authority from Constantinople, together with that of the Pope in Rome. However both places were a long way from Paris, which was besieged by the Franks; later, this tribe gave its name to France. Geneviève's prayers saved Paris from being destroyed by them, and her prayers were again effective on a later and more famous occasion.

A grim terror, affecting all lands as far as China and Greece, had overrun the known world. It was directed by a Hunnish king named Attila, known as the Scourge of God. He was a person of extraordinary authority, and recruited several tribes to fight for him in Europe. Among them were the Vandals, whose name meant much what it does today.

By 447, Attila had destroyed all civilisation between the Black Sea and the Mediterranean. In Constantinople the emperor, having been defeated three times, had retired behind the strong walls of his city and paid Attila large sums of money in tribute. Later the Pope, to save Rome, was to do the same. Having been given lands south of the Danube by the emperor, Attila then overran Gaul, the country which was later to be known as France. In Gaul, incredibly, the tide turned; he withdrew his armies, and a king named Theodoric defeated him at Châlons. This was said to have been brought about by the prayers of St. Geneviève, and it is certainly the first time this unconquerable man had retreated. He was not quite finished; he overran Italy, then died soon after his marriage with a beautiful princess of Burgundy. Meantime, the people of Paris were so grateful to Geneviève that after she died they made her their patron saint.

This remained the case until the French Revolution of 1793. Geneviève's relics, together with many other things which can never be replaced, were destroyed by the mob. There was no one left who dared prevent them. All who disagreed with them were either guillotined, or else had fled the country. A church built in

St. Geneviève's honour in 1764 was secularised under the name of the Panthéon.

Nevertheless relics are not everything. Remember that the power of prayer of St. Geneviève was enough to turn the armies of the Scourge of God.

Helen, Helena

There was of course the most beautiful woman in the world, Helen of Troy. It is possible that her fame had spread to Britain by 247 A.D., which is suggested as the year of the birth of St. Helena.

She is reputed to have been the daughter of a British king named Coël (Old King Cole was a merry old soul) and she certainly married a young Roman officer who was related to two emperors. His name was Constantius, and he was known as Chlorus because he had a greenish-pale complexion. Evelyn Waugh has written a novel, said to be his worst, called *Helena*, but I enjoyed it and so possibly may you. It gives a good idea of how in the days of the Roman Empire legions travelled immense distances along the good roads they had made, so it was perfectly possible for the son of the marriage, who became the emperor Constantine, to have been born in Naissus, now in Yugoslavia, if his mother travelled with her husband from Britain. However Helena's nationality is unimportant. What is important is that she later found the True Cross and the Holy Sepulchre.

Constantine was born in 279 A.D. At that time Christians were again being persecuted under Diocletian, and it is not known how Helena found out about the sect, but she must have kept her new beliefs from her husband although she possibly tried to influence her son in his boyhood; later he was taken away from her. However the seeds of the matter remained in his mind. He joined his father, who was fighting a tribe in France and later pacified Britain as far as it could be done, although he died at York (Eboracum) in 306, a year after he had become joint emperor. Constantine succeeded him, and Helena was given the title of Flavia Julia Helena, mother of Caesar. She was then in a strong position to influence her son and also to travel where she liked. In her old age she went to the Holy Land.

Waugh in his book gives Helena a good deal of downright common sense, and it was possibly this quality that led her to guess that the most triumphant pagan temple, that to Juno of the Victories, would deliberately have been built on the spot where Christ had been crucified almost three hundred years before. She caused workmen to dig beneath the foundations of the temple, and they found three crosses. It was established which one was the True Cross, and Helena brought it home by sea.

Home, at that point, was about to shift. Constantine had found Rome too cramped and unsuitable to be the capital of his expanding empire. He wanted to build a new one at Byzantium, and have it renamed Constantinople. This was done, and the Cross and the Crown of Thorns taken there with many other precious things; but before that happened Helena was dead.

Constantine was not yet a Christian; in fact he was not to be baptised till his deathbed. However he must have been aware that growing numbers of his men and officers secretly practised their religion despite the terrible punishments decreed by the former emperors; even his own father had sent St. Jerome into exile, and Jerome passed the time by writing a treatise on the Blessed Trinity. Whether or not it was convenient or the truth, Constantine said that he had seen a vision in the sky before his victory at the Milvian Bridge in 323. It was the Cross, and a voice said to Constantine 'In this sign conquer.' He won the battle, and thereafter, shortly before his mother died, declared Christianity the official religion of the empire. It was considered a surprising decision, and was almost certainly due to the influence of Helena, who died then, no doubt feeling that her work had been accomplished.

Hildegard

The media have adopted this amazing woman lately, although she was born in 1098. She was a person of so many gifts that even today, she would be noticed.

She was a sickly child, and not expected to live – certainly not to the age of 81, incredible for those days. She was given into the charge of Abbess Jutta, the count of Spanheim's sister, when she was 8. Her life was therefore expected not only to be short, but to be spent in the cloister.

At 15, Hildegard adopted the Benedictine habit. At 38, on the death of Jutta, she became abbess. Anyone might have thought that that was all, but things were only beginning.

Hildegard had always had visions, and one of the clearest of these is shown by her drawing of the Trinity as this was shown to her. It portrays God the Father as an orb, Christ the Son as a man standing below, haloed, and running between them on both sides a silver ribbon which is the Holy Spirit. All this bears out the *Filioque* clause which is still the chief cause of differences with the Orthodox Church. In Hildegard's vision it is clear that the Spirit proceeds from both Father and Son. Try to find a copy of the drawing.

Miracles happened during Hildegard's lifetime as well as after her death. One was the revelation to her of the place named Bingen on the river not far from Mainz. In 1147, Abbess Hildegard founded the convent of Rupertsberg, from which her letters were to make her famous all over the world, there.

Like all genuine persons, Hildegard was not convinced of her own certainty in any matter, and consulted her confessor, a monk named Godfrey, about the visions. The abbot of Mainz was informed and had a committee decide on them. Its decision was favourable, which means that Hildegard was not an hysteric. A later decision at Rome confirmed the findings. A learned monk named Volmar was appointed to be her secretary. The most famous of her writings is the *Scivias*, relating 26 visions. They deal with the relation between God, the creation and man. Hildegard would be called an environmentalist today; she was interested in natural history, plants and animals; she wrote two books on natural science and one on medicine. There was no end to her energy; she wrote a life of St. Rupert, another about a lesser known saint named Disibold; she wrote hymns and canticles, both the words and the music; you may hear some of them today on Radio 3. She wrote 50 homilies, using allegories, like Christ. For fun, she invented a language with 900 words and an alphabet of 23 letters. She also corresponded with kings and emperors, giving them advice; but she would talk to anyone, no matter how unimportant.

As she grew older, she began to travel through Germany and parts of Gaul, as France was still called. She was so frail by then that she had to be carried in a litter, unable to sit up. She died in extreme old age, and there were two processes begun in Rome at different times, remembering the miracles which took place during her life and at her tomb. However it is by her music that we best remember her, also the fact that she cared for the creation in times when there was even more animal cruelty than exists now. The abbess of Bingen knew that animals can love and trust, and she cared for them and for all plants and green things.

Her life was written by a monk named Theodoric, which is how we know more about her than the sound of her music.

Ida

There are two beatae named Ida. The first, Bl. Ida of Lorraine, died in 1113 on April 13th, her feast day. As a Lorrainer she would be brought up in the tradition of the great Abbess Hildegard of Bingen, who had travelled in her litter about the country in old age. Certainly Ida had a firm enough faith to pass it on to both her sons.

There is a curious tradition in her family. It was her father who, centuries later, gave Wagner the idea for his opera *Lohengrin*. Wagner sets the story in Brabant, but the Lorraine legend says a swan appeared, drawing in a boat a beautiful young man. He married the princess, but when her mother asked his name, the swan reappeared and removed the young man by water, and he was never seen again. The story may in fact have come from ancient Greece, where the god Zeus turned himself into a swan for Leda, the mother of Helen of Troy. Somebody in the Lorraine family may have known of this and that Mount Ida, in Greece, was where nymphs lived. Otherwise the name is unusual, although several of Ida's descendants were called after her. The swan was displayed on the family coat of arms for several centuries.

Ida married the Count of Boulogne and they had two sons, Godfrey and Baldwin. Both were fine soldiers and eventually took part in the first crusade. This was the only successful one, and after finding the Holy Lance deep in the earth before the altar at Antioch following a vision, the Christian armies took Jerusalem. Godfrey was elected king because of his bravery and his pious life. He would not however allow himself to be crowned or to take the name of king, only that of Defender of the Holy Sepulchre. 'I will not wear a crown of gold when my Saviour wore a crown of thorns,' he said. This kind of saying must surely have been taught him by his mother Ida.

Godfrey died before long, and Baldwin, the younger brother, succeeded him, this time as king. Countess Ida died five years before him. As everyone knows, the Latin kingdom of Jerusalem did not survive, and later crusades were unsuccessful in again taking the city. The person with the most success was St. Francis, who later persuaded the Sultan to let his friars become guardians of Christ's tomb.

Francis shared with the second Ida, a Cistercian nun who died in 1300, the honour of receiving the stigmata. This second Ida was known for her wonderful gifts of prayer, and was born near Louvain.

Joan

You will certainly have heard of St. Joan of Arc, but you may not have heard of St. Joan of France, who was a different person.

There are conflicting stories about the first – ask any Frenchman – and as I believe one of them rather than the other, I will only give a few facts here and you can try to find out the rest; you may decide to disagree, or not.

Certainly the English invaded France, and their early victories disheartened the French people. Later, a brave woman led the French to capture Orléans. She was known as the Maid of Orléans, and the surviving portrait of her is in a very old manuscript and shows her with long hair and a fitted dress that might almost be modern. She had earlier recognised the disguised Dauphin at Chinon and later, through her efforts, he became Charles VII. He may have been her half-brother according to one version, which is how she knew him. The other version says that she was a shepherdess who had had visions, and that her recognition of Charles was miraculous. Certainly anyone might have known him by his ugly nose.

Later, a young woman was tried for heresy after capture by the English, who had treated her abominably while in prison. They burnt her at the stake in Rouen in 1431. Today there is a church where the burning took place; it has flames painted on the glass and is built in a twisted form, like rising smoke. A statue to Joan of Arc, in gold, stands at the entrance to the town.

It is for you to decide whether there were two young women or only one. Read all you can about it.

The story of Joan of France is quite different. She was the granddaughter of Charles VII, and was a hunchback and cripple. She was so badly deformed that it is said the courtiers were told to hide her in their cloaks when her father, Louis XI, passed by. Joan was gentle and pious, but he could not love her. He married her to her cousin, Louis of Orléans, it was said in order that that branch of the family would have no children. Joan was made unhappy by Louis' mother, and Louis was not very kind to her either. She continued to make him a good and patient wife.

While Charles VIII, Joan's only brother, lived, her marriage continued. However Charles died of an accident in 1498, leaving no heir as his baby son was also dead. Louis decided to divorce Joan and to marry Charles' widow, Anne of Brittany. This was partly in order that Brittany might remain a part of France, but also because Louis, now he was king as Louis XII, wanted sons of his own to inherit; no woman could rule in France by Salic Law. The story is rather like that of Henry VIII a little later, and certainly Henry used the case of Louis' divorce to hasten his own.

Joan resisted the divorce, as Catherine of Aragon was to do; both women loved their husbands. However Joan was forced to accept it, and retired to a convent in Bourges, having refused to part with her wedding ring. Her nuns loved her greatly. She should be better known, and remembered when the name is chosen.

Anne of Brittany, like Anne Boleyn, gave her husband no sons either. One of their two daughters married the next king of France, another cousin, who became Francis I. In Brittany they still become angry if you call them French.

Laura

Laura, Laurentia, was a slave girl who converted her mistress, St. Palatias. Their story is something the same as that of the two young women saints Perpetua and Felicity (see article). However this martyrdom took place near Ancona in Italy, under the persecutions of Diocletian in 303.

Lucy

Lucy means 'light' in the way that the name Clare means 'clear light'. Both are pretty names, but this is not the only reason for choosing them. Their first holders were both brave women, though they lived almost a thousand years apart.

If you go into a church in Galicia, in northern Spain, you are almost certain to see a life-sized image of a beautiful young woman with dark hair. She is holding out a dish with two small round objects in it. They are her eyes, but the eyes are still in her head. The story, which is almost certainly added to what really happened, is that Lucy, a young woman of good family who lived in Syracuse in the year 304, had a young man who admired her and kept telling her how beautiful her eyes were. To show him that worldly things are unimportant, Lucy is said to have torn out her eyes and sent them to him on a dish. They were then miraculously restored to her.

Even for those days of extreme self-mortification and appalling tortured inflicted by others, I cannot think of the above story as anything but tall. What the people who related it are probably trying to point out is that Christ said 'If your right eye offend you, pluck it out and cast it from you.' He did not mean by this that anyone should blind themselves. He spoke in parables, which was the only way the crowds in Palestine could begin to understand what he was saying. What he meant was that if someone you dearly love persists in evil, it is better to rid yourself of them than to be corrupted by them. For Lucy to make herself blind for life and dependent on others would have been foolish, not saintly. However the statues of her are never those of a blinded woman and we may take it the young man learnt his lesson, except that the one in the real story did not.

The real story is that Lucy's mother had been ill and that Lucy prayed to St. Agatha, an earlier martyr, to cure her. St. Agatha not only did so, but appeared to Lucy in a vision to tell her to keep her purity, in other words not to marry the pagan bridegroom for whom her family had designed her. In fact the cure made Lucy's mother so grateful that she allowed her daughter, instead, to serve Christ by working among the poor.

The rejected pagan was angry at losing his bride, and denounced her as a Christian to the governor of Syracuse. He ordered Lucy to be thrown into prison, but when the guards came to take her away it was impossible to move her from the place where she stood. Presently they cast boiling oil over her and set her on fire. Lucy still refused to move, and in the end was killed in the customary way by stabbing her with a knife in the neck. She and her patroness St. Agatha were introduced together into the Canon of the Mass by Pope Gregory I; you may still hear the names read. It is partly by the life of Lucy that we remember Agatha, whose story was very similar in her day.

St. Lucy is a great favourite in Spain, and it is possible that devotion to her in England was renewed at the marraige of Philip II to Mary Tudor in 1554. The future St. Philip Howard was the king's godson, and in his later trials in the Tower under Elizabeth, his wife used to pray constantly to St. Lucy. Enough strength was given to her to lead a most saintly life of her own.

One of the Windward Islands is named after St. Lucy, and there is a famous song *Santa Lucia*. She is the patroness of eyesight. Relics of her were known to be in Abruzzo in the 8th century and later in Metz; an arm of hers was given to the emperor Henry III when he visited a German monastery. Earlier still, the crusaders had seen her relics in Constantinople.

We have no idea of what Lucy looked like, but a portrait of her is among the sixth-century mosaics in San Apollinare Nuovo in Ravenna. Beside her are two other women saints, the one on the right St. Cecilia, whose hair is fair. Lucy's is dark, which is probably correct as she was a Sicilian. Any images of her I have seen have dark hair and she is carrying, apart from the dish of eyes, a martyr's palm, a lamp, a book, or the fatal knife which killed her. Her relics were finally sent, in 1204, to Venice. Her feast day used to be the shortest day in the year, December 13th, as she is the patron of light; but not since the reformation of the calendar.

Madeleine, Magdalene

If your chosen name is Madeleine, Magdalene, Magdalen – all are forms of the same word, and it used to be pronounced Maudlin – it means that a woman named Mary came from a town called Magdala founded by the Greeks on the western shore of Lake Tiberias. It was still prosperous enough in the time of Christ to export luxury goods to Rome.

This woman had courage, and was not like the rest. You know some of her story from the Bible, also if you have been to see *Superstar*, which portrays her remarkably well. She does not come under the accepted forms of virgin or widow prescribed for most women saints, and she is still considered so far from respectable that her feast day, July 22nd, occurs when most people are away on holiday.

You all know the story of how she washed Christ's feet with her tears at last, then dried them with her long hair, after that using precious ointment from an alabaster jar to anoint his head. Before that she had been a woman of the town, a prostitute. St. Luke states that Christ had cast seven devils out of her. It is possible that she was the woman taken in adultery and brought in to be stoned. In St. John's Gospel she is stated to be the same person as Mary of Bethany, the sister of busy Martha, who was no help in the house, and of Lazarus who was raised from the dead. We do not know why, at that rate, she had left a good home to become a prostitute; there is a tale, probably invented, that she was betrothed to John, resented his taking away by Jesus and took to the streets in revenge. It is also possible that she was not the same person at all – scholars are still arguing about it – but it is interesting that it is St. John who states that she was Mary of Bethany.

Whoever she may have been, the legend of long hair persists and she is always shown with it flowing loose, lying at the foot of the Cross. I have also seen a very old French icon, in sepia ink, showing her covered in it from head to foot after having arrived on the coast of Provence with others after the Resurrection (see booklet on Sarah). The boat with the three Maries in it is still represented in churches in the Camargue, and St. Mary Magdalene's image is to be seen everywhere, including the old palace of the Popes in Avignon, holding the alabaster jar. It is possible that this may be a ciborium, an argument for women priests. Catholic Byzantines honour her as the Myrrh Bearer, and her planet, in Templar history, is that of Venus, whose six mathematical points indicate the six castles in France where the Shroud may have been kept while it was otherwise lost to history. All these legends and arguments perhaps do not matter, except for their interest, and for the fact that there is a strong memory of a woman saint who was so close to Christ that she was the first to see him after he had risen.

After coming to southern France and preaching there, she is said to have spent the last thirty years of her life in a cave above St. Baume. There is a tradition that when she died, St. Maximin gave her the last sacraments. There was another that her body was miraculously translated to Vézelay in Burgundy, where it was honoured for many centuries and where the first and second crusades were preached for the relief of the Holy Sepulchre. A blackened patella (knee-bone) said to be hers is among the relics at Westminster Cathedral. However lately her bones are said to have been discovered after all at Aix-en-Provence, which is more likely in the region where she died after so long.

Remembering the seven devils, rather than her repentance – respectability, once lost, is difficult to recover – places of restraint for fallen women, and madhouses, were called in the Middle Ages after St. Mary Magdalene. The fashionable Church of the Madeleine, in Paris, was erected in the nineteenth century on the site of one of these. The adjective 'maudlin' was used to describe self-pitying tears. Magdalen College, Oxford, is, as you know, pronounced Maudlin still in the old way, and its choir sings beautifully on May morning from the famous tower. Films and bizarre stories abound about this saint, including one with a conventional happy ending in Kashmir. If you see or hear any of these, remember only that this was the woman who loved Christ as a man; the song they give her in *Superstar* expresses the state of things perfectly, and is unforgettable. So is the *Noli Me Tangere*, the scene in the garden outside the empty tomb, by Fra Angelico; try to find a reproduction of it. If you go to visit Jerusalem, the church of St. Mary Magdalene is one of the most beautiful, just outside the Old Town near the place of Gethsemane. Magdala, a prosperous little place which exported wax, figs and oil to imperial Rome, certainly produced one of the most unusual women of all time, and a true and courageous saint to whom to pray. 'She has loved much, and much is forgiven her.'

That is a thought to remember.

Marcella

This brave woman, Marcella, was a very early saint, who lived in Rome. After the death of her husband she became a pupil of the famous St. Jerome, who wrote eleven letters to her; so she must have been an educated person able to read and write. She gathered a circle of women friends who used to meet in her house to study the Scriptures, possibly one of the first meetings of the kind.

This came to an end with the sack of Rome in 410 by the Goths. Marcella's house was not spared. They broke in looking for plunder, and finding nothing of any value thought she had hidden her riches. They scourged her to try to get her to reveal the hiding-place, unwilling to believe that there was nothing worth taking.

If the scourge used by the Goths was that of the Roman armies before them, it was the terrible metal-tipped, many-headed cat o'nine tails used on Christ. He is known, from examination of the Shroud, to have been already dying of haemorrhage, blood loss into the lungs, on the way to Calvary. It is no wonder that this gently bred Roman lady died of it. The murderers found nothing in the end, for all Marcella's possessions had been given to the poor. Her feast day, which should be more often remembered, is January 31st.

Margaret

If you have chosen the name Margaret, three saints spring to mind. One was a butcher's wife. The second was a queen. The third was a blind girl in Italy. There are many others, and some will be dealt with in separate articles. This one is about the queen.

St. Margaret of Scotland was born in Hungary in about 1045. The reason for her birth so far away goes back in history to fifty years before the Norman Conquest. She was descended from the old English royal line of Alfred the Great. The heir was known as the Atheling, in something the same way as the heir to the throne today is called the Prince of Wales. Margaret is therefore sometimes called Margaret Atheling, although there were no surnames in those days. Her brother, Edgar the Atheling as he was known, should have inherited the crown of England, but never did.

Long before, by 1016, Margaret's great-grandfather, King Ethelred II, had married twice. By his first marriage, to a lady named Ithelgina, he had a son Edmund, who grew up to be such a brave fighter that he was known as Edmund Ironside. His father the king was very different. The name Ethelred, in Old English, means Noble Counsel, but this king was nicknamed Ethelred Unred, which means the Ill-Advised. He certainly did most things the wrong way. For a long time, since before the days of Alfred who had conquered them, the Danes, sea pirates and pagans, had raided parts of England, doing much harm and sometimes settling there. King Ethelred made the mistake of trying to buy them off with money instead of fighting them, so all that happened was that they kept coming back for more and continued their raids. Edmund Ironside, the king's son, took a great army against their leader, Cnut. The two sides fought all day, but neither won and the battle was drawn. Then Edmund issued a challenge to Cnut to fight a duel with him. The two young men fought, again all day, and once more the result was drawn, one fighter having proved as good as the other. In the end the two exhausted leaders agreed to divide England up between them, each to rule half. For only a few days, therefore, Edmund Ironside was king of half England. Sadly, he was already dying. A traitor named Edric of Kent had come up behind him after the duel, and had thrust a spear into his back. Ironside was carried to Oxford, where, a few days later, he died.

His two sons, both children, had to flee the country, which was by then in the power of Cnut. Shortly the Dane became king of all England and married King Ethelred's widow and second wife, Emma of Normandy. It is important to remember about this lady.

Cnut made not a bad king, and became enough of a Christian to make a pilgrimage to Rome to visit the Pope. When Cnut died his son by Emma succeeded, then, when he died also, the surviving son of Emma and Ethelred was recalled from Normandy to claim the English crown. You have certainly heard of him; he became known as King Edward the Confessor, but it is not generally known that he spoke French and had many Norman habits, like this mother. He was a saintly man and, shortly after his death, was canonised and was for a time England's favourite saint.

Meantime, the young sons of Edmund Ironside had grown up at the court of Hungary. One died, but the other, Edward the Stranger, married a Hungarian bride whose name was probably Agatha and who may have been the king's daughter. They had three children before Edward the Stranger died. The children were named Margaret, Christina and Edgar the Atheling. The last should as stated have been England's king, but nobody remembered about him and he was never a fighter like his grandfather Ironside.

Now that Cnut was dead, it was safe for the royal children to return to the Confessor's court. They were made welcome by Edward and his queen Edith, and were brought up by them in such piety that Christina later became an abbess. Margaret also wanted to become a nun, but events decided otherwise.

Perhaps the widowed Agatha had hoped that her son Edgar would be named as King Edward's successor, but the throne was promised instead to the queen's brother Harold. As everyone has heard, Harold, the last Saxon king, was killed fighting bravely at the Battle of Hastings in 1066 against William, duke of Normandy, who claimed England partly by reason of Emma, who had been his great-aunt, and for other reasons.

The Confessor had died in 1066, and in that year Agatha and her family thought it best to return to Hungary for safety, and took ship. What happened then has been described as the will of God. A storm drove the ship off course, and the fugitives landed instead in Scotland. There the king, Malcolm III, a widower with two young sons, greatly desired to marry Margaret, who had grown up into a beautiful young woman. However she had decided, as said already, to become a nun, and was unwilling. At last, having been persuaded that she could do great good for the Church in Scotland, she was married to King Malcolm in 1067. It does not sound to us a reason for marrying if one has decided not to, but in fact the couple were very happy. King Malcolm was known as Ceann Mór in Gaelic, which means not Big Head as many think, but Great Chief. There were many races in Scotland which in former times had obeyed different chiefs; there were the Gaels or Celts, the Picts, who spoke a different language, and the men of Moray whose blood was mostly Norse. In Galloway, in the south-west, they almost thought of themselves as a separate kingdom and did as they chose. A strong king was needed, and Margaret herself made a strong queen.

Margaret

She built a chapel at Dunfermline and furnished it with many rich and beautiful things, including the famous Black Rood of Scotland, a great jewelled crucifix which she had probably brought from Hungary. The palace nearby was filled by her with brightly coloured hangings and weaving; she brought splendour to the bleak country, but also made many reforms, not all of which were popular. The observance of Sunday had been forgotten about, also the keeping of Lent. Margaret reintroduced these, and the other things which had been brought long before by St. Ninian in the fifth century and continued by St. Columba and St. Kentigern, who met once at a green place called Glasgow. The banner of Columba, called the Brecbennoch, was still produced on great occasions. Margaret set herself to reform remote places such as the far-off island of Iona, where Columba had lived on a diet of nettles and would not even allow cows on the island to give milk to the community he had founded. This however was long before.

Malcolm Ceann Mór and his queen had eight children, six sons and two daughters. There were already two sons of Malcolm's by his first marriage, one called after himself and the other after his father King Duncan, the 'gracious Duncan' of Shakespeare's *Macbeth*. However the real Duncan had not been an old man when he was killed fairly in battle by the real Macbeth, who had reigned for seventeen years and was then killed in turn by Malcolm in a later battle, as stated in the play. Margaret's sons were named, therefore, for the Atheling line; Edward, Edgar, Ethelred, Edmund, and then Alexander and at last, David. The girls were Edith, after the Confessor's queen, and Mary for the Mother of God. It was unusual in those times to use the name. Margaret wanted her sons to be monks and her daughters nuns, but in this respect she and the king did not agree; he once tore a veil from young Edith's head and later, when she was with her abbess aunt Christina at Romsey, she used to jump on her veil, as said elsewhere. She married the Conqueror's son Henry I and changed her name to Matilda, becoming known as the Good Queen Maud. Her sister Mary married the count of Boulogne. However some of the brothers carried out their mother's wishes; Ethelred became an abbot and Edmund a monk in the end, and three of the other sons reigned as kings in Scotland.

Meantime, King Malcolm built his wife a little stone chapel against the outer wall of Edinburgh Castle; it is still there, and the cold of the stones in a Scottish winter must have made it difficult to kneel and pray. Margaret however prayed a great deal, and early in the marriage her husband noticed that she always went out very early in the morning. He thought she must be going to meet a lover, and one day followed her with drawn sword. He came upon her secretly praying in a cave, for him and for his kingdom. After that he helped her in every way in her reforms of the Church, which she brought back to obedience to the Pope. She also insisted on obedience from her own children, and told their tutors not to spare the rod!

William the Conqueror meantime ruled in England, and as his rule was cruel King Malcolm, perhaps hoping also to be rid of his brother-in-law the Atheling, fitted him out with ships and arms and rich clothing to try to regain his inheritance in the south. However with the Atheling's usual ill-luck, a storm sank the ships and everything was lost. In the end William the Conqueror decided that the Atheling was so harmless there was no need to worry about him. By the end, Margaret would have had reason to be grateful to her brother; but she was dead.

Malcolm and Margaret died within four days of each other. The king was betrayed and killed at Tynemouth in Northumbria in 1093, along with Margaret's eldest son Edward. Margaret was ill at the time, and when she heard the news she died of grief. A brother of King Malcolm prepared to seize the throne, and Margaret's sons carried her body secretly out of Edinburgh Castle in a thick mist. They buried her in Dunfermline, where, later, bones thought to be her husband's were brought and entombed also. The two girls and the younger boys – David was very small — were hurried south out of danger to the English court by the Atheling, their uncle. The girls were placed with their strict aunt Christina, but David grew up at the court of Henry I and married a great heiress. This made for good relations between Scotland and England when David became king of Scots and his sister Edith married Henry. King David I built nine glorious abbeys in Scotland, mostly on the Borders; their ruins can still be seen. They cost a great deal to build, for like his mother David grudged nothing. He was a saintly man, and a later king of Scots remarked sourly that he had been 'a sair sanct to the croun.' However David was never canonised, though his mother Queen Margaret was so in 1251, in the reign of her great-great-great-grandson Alexander III. Her body, after more than 150 years, was found to be incorrupt, with beautiful fair hair. When they tried to move the coffin to the grand new tomb, it could not be lifted until that of King Malcolm was brought also. This may not be the miracle it was said to be; Celtic Scots still resented the influence of the Saxon queen and may have arranged that the coffin refused to move till his did. In the meantime, bones thought to be more certainly those of King Malcolm were found at Tynemouth, where he had died. However Margaret of Scotland, with her reforms and her charities to the poor and sick, is certainly a saint even if everyone did not like her. This happens to saints as well as to the rest of us.

Martha

Jesus had three friends he liked to visit in Bethany, a place not far from Jerusalem. They were a brother and two sisters, and it is possible that they came from the north like himself. They seem to have been people of substance; certainly they had prepared a rock-cut tomb for themselves, as was the custom with richer families. They were also able to entertain Jesus hospitably in their house.

About the brother, Lazarus, we know very little, except that his sisters were devoted to him and grieved when he died. About the two sisters we know much more: we know, for instance, that they were quite different from one another.

Martha was undoubtedly the one in charge of the house. She was probably rather bossy. She was the kind of person who has to have everything as it ought to be, and such people can be hard to live with (see the article on her sister Mary in *Madeleine*). On the other hand her way of serving Jesus was to give him the best she could in every way, taking all kinds of trouble about the cooking, the wine, the cups, the placings at table. She bustled about, while Mary sat and listened to Jesus. Which would you have done? It depends whether you are a Mary or a Martha. We know what Jesus had to say on the subject, and perhaps Martha was caused to think. However it is possible to be active for God and to think, or pray, at the same time.

When Lazarus died, it was Martha who ran out to meet Jesus, after he had delayed coming for four days. 'Lord, if you had been here my brother would not have died.' This shows an almost childlike faith, the kind of unquestioning belief which people like Martha adopt if they adopt it at all. Mary, we are told, sat still in the house; even then, she had more understanding. If Jesus had delayed, she knew he had reasons. Martha still did not understand. 'Lord, I know he will rise again at the last day.' This is a literal belief, the kind taught to every Jewess. Nobody can have been more astonished than Martha when at the words 'Lazarus, come forth,' her brother walked in his gravecloth wrappings up the many steps deep down to the tomb, and came out alive into the daylight. We hear no more of her making any fuss. The next, which is legend, is that after the Resurrection she went with some of the other women to France, and is remembered there; many churches are built and named for her. There is also a gate in the Vatican named the Porta Santa Marta. Christ's eager hostess is not underrated or forgotten.

Lazarus himself is said to have gone to Cyprus, and was never known to smile again, having passed through death. There is an order named after him which does practical good concerning the sick. This would have pleased his sister Martha.

Matilda

St. Matilda was of Saxon descent. She was the wife of the emperor Henry I, known as the Fowler. In those days Popes and emperors had not yet begun to disagree, and Matilda was free to carry out her works of charity while her husband waged wars against the Slavs, Bohemians, Hungarians and Danes. Matilda promoted the religious education of children and greatly helped the poor. She also built many churches and decorated them with her own embroidery. Immediately on her death in 968, the year before St. Olga's, she was declared a saint with rather more reason! For generations royal princesses were named after her; perhaps the most easily remembered is William the Conqueror's queen, Matilda of Flanders. Other queens, with names like Edith and Alice, adopted the name Matilda by popular request. The saint's feast day is on March 14th.

Monica

The name Monica – it is sometimes spelt with two n's – is a pretty one, and perhaps you have chosen it for that reason. It may also be the case that you know St. Monica had a famous son, St. Augustine of Hippo.

Monica was a Christian who married a pagan, Patricius, about the year 350. They lived in a small town called Tagetes in Numidia, North Africa, not far from Carthage. Carthage had been a powerful city once, but had lost its final war with Rome – there were three of them – and by the time of Monica's birth in 332 was what we would today call a university town, no longer of the first importance.

Patricius and Monica had three children, Navigius, Augustine and Perpetua. The girl was certainly named after the young martyr who had died in Carthage a century and a half earlier. This shows that Monica had some influence over her husband, although the marriage was not altogether a happy one. Before Patricius died in 371, however, Monica had converted him to Christianity.

By then, it seemed almost too late to do anything about Augustine. At the age of sixteen, the year before his father died, he had entered the university of Carthage and became one of its most brilliant students, winning the first place in the school of rhetoric. Two years later, he met a young woman.

This unknown woman has my sympathy. She bore Augustine a son, whom he called Adeodatus, the gift of God. He may have remembered his mother's teachings, but about that time he was enthralled with Cicero's writings and speeches, which he thought were much better than Scripture. Meantime he and the young woman lived together, with their son, for fourteen years. Today they would be called husband and wife in common law, but they were not married. It is possible that the young woman was a slave, which meant that a man of good family could not marry her. Whoever she was, her feelings do not seem to have been greatly considered in the course of events.

Augustine then became, and remained for nine years, a Manichaean. These were members of a non-Christian sect which believed in Mani, a visionary who had in the end been executed by one of the Persian emperors. His form of religion no doubt attracted Augustine because of its diversity; it includes all kinds of subjects including anthropology and botany, predicts the end of the world in fire, and meantime cautions its elect not to touch meat or wine and if possible, to be celibate. To describe himself as given over to passion at this period, as Augustine later did, seems odd to our way of thinking; but all his mother knew was that he was lost to her faith and showed signs of turning out like his father.

She tried to arrange a suitable marriage for Augustine, which shows how little she really understood his mind. At one point he left her behind on purpose while he sailed for Rome, telling her the ship sailed later than it did. That was in the year 383, and already his mind was again changing.

It is certain that St. Ambrose, then bishop of Milan, helped Augustine convert himself to belief in Christ rather than in Mani. When Monica at last arrived from Africa, it was to find that, far from desiring a suitable marriage, her son had been so impressed by the bishop's arguments that he was already considering baptism for himself and Adeodatus, and had taken a vow of celibacy, or else renewed it. He was particularly impressed by the story of St. Anthony of Egypt, whose experiences in the desert had persuaded two imperial officers to enter a monastery.

On Easter Eve, 387, he and Adeodatus were baptised by St. Ambrose. It is said that on that occasion the Te Deum was composed. Monica, feeling that her life's work was complete, set out for Africa, but died at Ostia before reaching home.

The boy Adeodatus died soon also. Augustine, having become a famous teacher and theologian, was ordained and became bishop of Hippo, not far from his birthplace. His most famous writings are the *Confessions*, written in the year St. Ambrose died; also the *City of God*. His sister Perpetua, called after the saint, founded an Augustinian convent at Tagetes. Augustine himself died while the Vandals, an invading tribe, were besieging Hippo in 430. His mother's body had been buried first at Ostia, then was removed to a monastery near Arras in France, which caused her cult to spread in that country. Other relics are in the church of St. Augustine in Rome. St. Monica's feast day is May 4th.

Olga

St. Olga, who died in 969, is shown in hopeful leaflets as a young, beautiful and starry-eyed princess. In fact she was the tough old widow of Prince Igor of Kiev, probably herself a peasant. She governed, ably but with great cruelty, the province after Igor's death, which she avenged. She had to do other things which seem to us savage – once she buried 35 ambassadors alive in a boat – but it has to be remembered that for a woman to rule in those times she had to be ruthless. Even two centuries later the English would not accept the rule of one. Olga at least preserved the province intact for her son and for her grandson, St. Vladimir.

Olga was received into the Church fairly late in life, after a ceremony of great pomp which named her Female Exarch of Russia. The ceremony took place in Constantinople, in the presence of the emperor, and Olga brought with her a large train of converts which included four interpreters. It is doubtful whether Christianity meant to her what it means to us. Even by her grandson's time it was a question of becoming one or else having your head chopped off. Mass baptisms took place, accordingly, in Russian rivers.

Nevertheless Olga did immense service to Russia in starting to make it what it became by the end; a deeply mystical Christian country, the quality of whose religion has survived repression and, worse, governmental imitation during the communist régime. The latter deceived few, and by now there is an open resurgence of faith in Russia.

The name of Olga was adopted by the imperial rulers, and among them was the eldest daughter of the last Tsar, Grand Duchess Olga, murdered at Ekaterinburg in 1918 with most of her family.

Rose

St. Rose of Lima is the patron saint of Peru, all of America, the Indies and the Philippines. She is the first saint of the New World.

She was born on 20th April 1586. Her father was a Spanish conquistador. As we know, the Spanish conquest was very cruel. He married a young girl named Maria de Oliva. His own name was de Flores, which is strange when we think how easily his daughter grew flowers.

When the child was born, she was christened Isabel. However an Indian maid said that the baby, born at Pentecost, was so beautiful she was like a rose. Her mother permitted the use of this name and the little girl was later confirmed in it, calling herself presently Rosa de Santa Maria because of her devotion to the Blessed Virgin. She also took St. Catherine of Siena as her model and copied her in many ways.

Even as a child, Rose fasted and underwent mortifications. She would have liked to take vows in a convent, but this was not permitted. However she was able to enter the Third Order of St. Dominic at the age of 20, and thereafter wore the habit and veil. Her mother liked her to wear a crown of roses, and was obeyed; but under it the girl secretly wore a crown of thorns. When she had been small she had built herself a little hermitage in the garden, and she spent much of her time there and in growing her flowers, which she sold for the relief of the poor children whom she began to tend, together with old people, in an infirmary she set up in the house. This was the first time anything of the kind had happened in Peru, and soon it came to the notice of the Inquisition, who questioned Rose. They could only report that she seemed to be 'directed by impulses of grace.'

She had mystical experiences, but was unable to write them down. It was widely believed in Lima that she had saved the people there from being attacked by pirates. For this and for her charity she was much beloved.

She died on August 24th, 1617, having prophesied the date of her death exactly. Such crowds thronged the funeral that it could not take place for some days, and at first Rose was buried in the church of the Dominicans, as she had requested. Later her body was moved to the cloister, then into church; today it rests in front of an altar in the crypt.

Her cause was introduced at Rome in 1634, and four years later she was beatified. She was canonised in 1671 under Clement IX. Although she is less well known over here, few in South America will have failed to hear of her.

Sarah

Most people will tell you that there is no such person as a saint named Sarah. They are wrong.

Besides the famous wife of Abraham in the Old Testament, who with her husband entertained the Trinity, and later gave birth in old age to Isaac as promised, there is a second owner of the name who was probably alive in the time of Christ. She is remembered in a particularly special part of southern France, the Camargue. She is the patron saint of gipsies.

That part of the land is washed by the tideless Mediterranean, the oldest sea in the world, whose southern edge reaches Africa. Long ago, after the Crucifixion, three women set out from the Holy Land in a boat. They were Mary Magdalene (see our article), Mary Jacoby, mother of James; and Mary Salomé, the kinswoman of Our Lady. With them came their servant, Sarah. If this is a myth, it is a very beautiful one. Sarah had at first been left behind – perhaps the three others were pursued – but prayed to be allowed to go with them. A miraculous cloak floated on the water, Sarah walked on it out to the boat, and joined her three patrons.

They sailed for many days, then came to a land with strange white horses which love the sea and always return to it. There were lambs which fed on rosemary, which grows wild on these shores and gives a sweet flavour to their flesh when eaten. The people and their language were different from that spoken further north. At some point where the women had landed, a town was built and called Les-Trois-Saintes-Maries-de-la-Mer, the three saints from the sea called Mary.

St. Mary Magdalene made many conversions there, and died long afterwards. There are many statues of her in the Camargue, but only one of Sarah, who became a saint as well. In the little underground chapel at Les-Trois-Maries there is a life-sized figure of her, dark-eyed, smiling, and wearing a red shawl. Each year on her feast day, May 24th, gipsies come from all over the world, camp in the surrounding fields and hear Mass in the chapel, which contains saints' bones in a reliquary. Even when it is empty again, the chapel smells of campfire smoke, onions and gipsies. It has such a happy feeling that although nothing more is known about St. Sarah, or Sara, you have chosen the right name and even if you are not a gipsy, she will protect you.

Sophia

There is a ridiculous story about a Christian widow named Sophia who had three daughters called Faith, Hope, and Charity, all of whom were put to death by the emperor Hadrian. It may be an improving tale, but it did not happen. The following did.

The word Sophia, in Greek, means wisdom. As you know, there is a Book of Wisdom in the Bible, worth reading for its beautiful prose as well as for its common sense. Apart from this, there is a famous basilica in Constantinople named Hagia Sophia, Holy Wisdom. Sadly, although it was built for Christian worship, it is now a mosque; but the banner of the Crescent displayed beneath its great dome does not look as if it belonged there. Having taken off your shoes and left them outside, you may tread over the old stones of the floor, and there you will see a series of tiny crosses, worked into the stone. They are the places where ancient processions used to pause at certain parts of the liturgy. It is impossible to forget that the building was once the greatest Christian church in the world, at least the eastern world of the later emperors.

The builder of Hagia Sophia was the emperor Justinian I. He is remembered also for his Codex of laws. He built many other churches in Constantinople, including the beautiful Blue Mosque; also, he surrounded the city with towers for fortification, which kept it for many centuries from falling to enemy hordes. Go to Constantinople if you can.

If you call yourself Sophia, therefore, you have no patron saint except the Holy Spirit, prayers to whom are among the best of all.

Susanna, Susan

There is a story of Susanna and the elders in the Old Testament, but although she was a chaste woman she is not spoken of as a saint. There is however a saint of the name, who lived much later. She was born in about 840 in the rich city of Constantinople. Today she is remembered by a market in Rome, next to the Santo Spirito arcades, where they sell coral necklaces. However if you ask anyone buying a necklace about St. Susanna, they probably will not know. The reason is that she spent 50 years in solitude.

There are people who choose this, and who prefer to be alone. It does not mean that they are lonely. You may have heard the expression 'blessed solitude'. Most people cannot understand the wish for it. Nowadays such women are called anchoresses, and there are some in the heart of London.

Susanna must have found Constantinople noisy and distracting. She had a mother who was determined to marry her off. We have all met such mothers, and while they may suit some daughters they do not suit others. Susanna endured this life until she was 28, then fled to Leucadia, where from then on she lived alone in a cave. She is said to have been much beloved by the people of the district. She died in 918, at a great age for those days; work it out.

Teresa

Two most famous saints named Teresa are the Spaniard, St. Teresa of Avila, born in 1515, and Ste. Thérèse of Lisieux in Normandy, born much nearer our own time in 1873. Both were Carmelites.

Teresa of Avila – her family's name was de Cepeda – was a person of immense energy. She was beautiful, with great dark eyes and a white skin found incorrupt many years after her death. There is a portrait of her taken in middle life, showing the lines from nose to mouth induced by penances and her unending taxing of herself in her cause of reform of the Order.

When she was a child, Teresa and her small brother ran away to try to walk to Rome. They did not manage it, but later on, when she was 18, Teresa became a Carmelite nun.

She found that the rule had become very lax. As she was a woman who never did things half-heartedly, she set out to try to reform it. At first this made her unpopular; people do not want their comfortable lives made uncomfortable. However Teresa achieved her object in the end, and finally established what was virtually a separate, much stricter order, the Discalced Carmelites. She was helped greatly by her friendship with St. John of the Cross. It may give some idea of the difficulties to be faced when it is mentioned in passing that he was kidnapped and held in a tower for three days and nights by Teresa's opponents!

St. Teresa had the highest degree of mystical experience. Several times she levitated four feet above the floor while praying; her alarmed nuns tried in vain to hold her down. Teresa also had her famous ecstatic vision, which has been made the subject of a sculpture by Bernini, of white marble and gold, at the entry to St. Peter's, Rome.

She wrote a great deal, letters of advice and exhortation. She had a great many wise things to say. One is 'Let nothing disturb you, nothing frighten you. All things pass; God does not change. Patience achieves everything. Whoever has God lacks nothing. God alone suffices.'

Ste. Thérèse was the same and yet different. Physically she was not as strong. She was the youngest of three sisters, and her mother Zélie died early. Thérèse was brought up by her father, a watchmaker named Louis Martin, in Alençon where she had been born, and her greatest treat was to be taken to church. She was a very pretty little girl, with long fair curls and delicate features. From an early date – probably as soon as she knew about them – she was determined to enter the Carmelite convent at Lisieux, a few miles further north, near Caen. As though she knew she had not long to live, she wanted to enter it early. She persuaded her father to take her to see the Pope, knelt and appealed to him personally to allow her to enter the Carmelite Order at fifteen. The prescribed age was sixteen, but so greatly impressed was Leo XIII by the child's sincerity that he agreed. Thérèse entered Carmel, and began a tough life quite different from the one she had led at home. There are no physical comforts in a Carmel, and Thérèse slept on a hard pallet, swept floors and washed clothes in the laundry as well as sharing in the prayers and liturgy.

She had had certain visions as a child – one was of little devils dancing on a dustbin – and in a little while she was ordered by her Superior to write all these down. We can read them today, and can see her drawings of flowers. She had taken the name of Sister Thérèse of the Child Jesus, as she had always had a particular devotion to the Christ Child. Her 'Little Way' – life in an enclosed convent can mean many irritations which would not trouble us outside because we can get away from them – was to offer up everything to God, even the maddening rattle of a rosary or the splashing of water on one's snowy habit and cloak. Some of the entries make amusing reading.

However Thérèse was not well, although she said nothing of it till it was no longer possible to hide it. She died of tuberculosis in 1897, aged only 24. 'I want to spend my heaven in doing good on earth,' she had said, and her answer to the prayers of many makes her a favourite among present-day saints. She asked that her body should not be incorrupt, and this prayer was granted, unlike her great precursor Teresa of Avila, who had died in 1582.

Theodora, Dorothy

Theodora, Dorothea, Dorothy, all mean the same thing; the gift of God. There was a famous Byzantine empress named Theodora, whose portrait, with her husband Justinian, you can see in the famous mosaics of Ravenna; she is almost weighed down with pearls and embroidery.

Dorothea, or Dorothy, was a young Christian martyr, like so many, in the time of Diocletian. Her name is connected with flowers, Like St. Rose of Lima. Christ himself loved flowers and knew their names; you remember he said 'Consider the lilies of the field; they toil not, nor do they spin; yet Solomon in all his glory was not arrayed like one of these.' Our Lady is often portrayed with lilies, which mean purity, and after the Assumption the place where she had lain is by tradition found to have been filled with lilies.

You have just read about St. Thérèse of Lisieux, who is known as the Little Flower. Her statues are generally shown with roses, and there were golden roses on the feet of the beautiful lady who appeared at Lourdes. The people who look after the flowers in church are doing an important job; think what it would be like without any, and remember that, like the name Dorothy, flowers are the gift of God as well.

Ursula

A legend is a story which is based on remembered truth. In the passing of time, and in the telling, it gathers details which were not there in the first place or which may have been taken from similar legends. Such a story is that of St. Ursula and her 11,000 virgins.

It has been argued that Ursala could not have existed because all her name means is *ursus*, a bear. In fact this goes to prove her probable existence, as the bear was the symbol of the British Celts.

The symbol was applied to Arthur, the great Celtic hero of legend and who was known as the Bear of Britain. He fought the Saxons, who in early times, when they were still pagan, invaded this country and drove the earliest Christians mostly westwards. Many of these Celts fled to Wales, Cornwall and Brittany. This can be proved even today, as a Welshman can understand a Breton although the native speech of the Cornish has been lost. Later the Saxons also were converted to Christianity, but you will agree that a short dark Welshman is very different from a tall fair Englishman, even in the way he thinks.

It is possible that one of these mass flights, or migrations as they are known, occurred at about the same time as a daughter of the king of Cornwall set out, it is said unwillingly, to marry a bridegroom her father had chosen for her. It meant crossing the sea to Brittany. Possibly eleven handmaidens were chosen to go with her, but not 11,000; for one thing there would not have been enough transport! A migration, however, might have voyaged in many coracles or small boats made of leather on wood and rowed with oars.

Meantime the unwilling bride – and this is almost certainly invention – is said to have chosen the longest way round to reach her bridegroom, by way of Rome. (Look at the map and you will agree that this is unlikely.) On return, she and her maidens encountered a storm and were shipwrecked at the mouths of the Rhine. This part is probably true. The barbarians there carried off or killed the maidens, and Ursula herself, if this was her name, received a proposal of marriage from the Hunnish prince, their leader. She rejected his advances, and he slew her with his sword. This is an echo of the many Christian martyrs who died in defence of their chastity. A church to the memory of St. Ursula was built at Cologne as early as the 4th and 5th centuries, and Cologne is on the Rhine.

The Breton version of the story is this. A king named in recorded history, Conan Mériadech – the word Conan means 'king', and Mériadech may well have been Murdoch, and the king a Scot who had earlier fled to Brittany from the Saxons – having carved out a kingdom for himself, reigned many years. He was so zealous a Christian, in the terms of those days, that he killed all the Druids of the country who refused to be baptised. Nine Druid priestesses fled to the Isle of Sein, and were known to help sailors have safe voyages by the spells they cast. They were also said to be able to turn themselves into animals. Conan Mériadech's men finally went out to the island, and killed all nine. For many centuries the island was accursed and uninhabited.

Conan Mériadech's first wife having died, he wanted to marry again. He had heard that the king of Cornwall had a beautiful daughter, and asked for her hand. The ship sailed as already related, but without going to Rome; it was shipwrecked at the Rhine mouths and the above fate befell the (probably) eleven handmaidens and Ursula, the princess.

However paintings and carvings of 11,000 virgins on board ship abound and are very beautiful. So is the cathedral at Cologne; and the order of Ursuline nuns was founded in 1537.

Veronica

If you have chosen the name Veronica, it belonged to nobody in the first place. The word is in fact what is known as a metonymy. (Look up the dictionary.) It may mean Vera Icon, True Image. If you know Greek, its form is Bepvíkn, or Bepovíkn, and can be pronounced Beronica, Berenice, Vernice, or even Venice. The letters b and v are interchangeable, as in modern Spanish – the duke of Alva could spell his name Alba, depending on how he felt.

The legend is that when Christ was on his way to Calvary, carrying his cross and in great pain and weariness, a woman in the crowd wiped the sweat and blood from his face with a cloth. Handkerchiefs were unknown in those days, so she may have used her veil; all women wore one. Later it is said that the imprint of Christ's face was found on the cloth. It, or one like it, was venerated in the 10th and 11th centuries at Rome; but there is far more to the story.

We know that the Shroud, the long linen cloth believed to be the one folded above and below Christ's dead body meantime till the Sabbath should be over, was kept folded carefully in a shrine in Constantinople, where it was seen by the crusaders. They would see only the face. The same thing happened later at Edessa, where the folded Shroud was kept for many years in a cavity in a wall. Perhaps it was not realised that the body also had left marks on the parts hidden by the folds, and the legend grew of the Vera Icon, or Vernacle, the Sacred Face. Artists who saw the cloth drew images of Christ as the long-haired bearded man we know, differently from the very early images which where made by painters and mosaic-workers who had never seen him or met anyone who had done so. Most of these show a clean-shaven man with short fair hair, except for a profile in the Catacombs said to have been painted by St. Luke. That shows a bearded man with dark hair, and a profile which matches that on the Shroud after scientific photography. Scientists have worked on every aspect of the Shroud, and the only flaw in the evidence has been that of carbon dating. This may well be the case because of the effects of fire at a time when the Shroud was locked up in a silver casket. The gases given off by the burning silver would affect the carbon in the linen threads, and also the Resurrection itself, which may have been a kind of nuclear explosion, would make carbon dating inaccurate after a lapse of time.

However there is still another clue, this time straight from the Gospels. You will remember that when the women came back with spices to the tomb (they would also be carrying linen bandages to wrap the dead body finally, rather like the swaddling bands used at birth) and found the tomb empty, they ran back to tell the others while Mary Magdalene stayed on at the tomb, weeping, then saw Our Lord in the garden. Presently the disciples came, and Peter went right into the tomb. He found not only the cloth which had covered the body, neatly folded, but a second cloth which had been round the head, folded separately by itself. This may be the Vernacle. There was certainly some such relic seen or remembered, and numberless paintings and embroideries from the Middle Ages show the face of the same man. You will see, from the painted glass head in the Resurrection Window in Shelton, Norfolk, that the sixteenth-century painter must have seen the Shroud or a close copy. Look at the placing of the wound from the high priest's servant, the first received, and the swelling of the face on that side as a result, so that the eyes themselves look uneven. Compare it with the Shroud face and remember that no one had seen anything but dull marks on linen until the mid-nineteenth century, when an Italian photographer developing a negative of the Shroud got the surprise of his life.

If, therefore, you have chosen the name Veronica, do not be disappointed that it is not the name of a person. The real name of the woman said to have wiped Christ's face is unimportant; the important thing is that she had the bravery and compassion to come out of the hostile crowd and aid a criminal on his way to public execution, whether or not she knew who he was already. It was a simple act of mercy which may have brought its own great reward, as such acts often can.

Winifred

Winifred was a niece of St. Beuno, and lived in Wales. This was a place of many saints, but her story is particularly famous.

Her shrine is called Holywell in Clwyd, and even one of the sandbanks in the neraby river has been called Holywell Bank. The place was one of the most often visited shrines in the Middle Ages, and even as late as the reign of Henry VII, father of the destroyer of shrines, a stone shelter was built by the king and his mother, Lady Margaret Beaufort, to protect the ancient well where the saint's bloodstains are still said to be seen at the bottom, on the stones.

Winifred had been taught the Christian faith by her uncle, and was a devout girl, very beautiful. She attracted the notice of a young man named Caradog of Hawarden. When Winifred refused his suit he followed her, and in anger cut off her head. Legend says that the ground then swallowed him up. As for the head, it fell in the stream. Winifred's uncle St. Beuno retrieved it and set it back on her neck again. She came back to life with only a narrow red ring about her neck to show what had happened.

She was so grateful to her uncle for restoring her to life that she promised to spin and weave him a cloak each year, float it down the water to wherever he might be, and pray that it was delivered. It seems to us a chancy way to deliver anything, but shows the power of these early saints' prayers that it happened. Winifred herself entered the convent at Gwytherin in Denbigh, which like most in those days was for men as well as women. After some time the abbot died, then the abbess, and Winifred was chosen to succeed.

The well where her head had fallen became well known, and it is still said that the moss growing about it gives off a scent of frankincense. You may still visit it at the place in Wales called Holywell, not far from Flint.

Zita

St. Zita was a servant girl who secretly gave away her mistress's food to the poor. Once she was nearly caught giving away beans, and the pot was miraculously filled again. Another time she gave away her mistress's fur coat, and an angel handed it back at the door. In spite of all this, Zita is known to have said that a servant ought to do her job well. This applies to anything we do. Zita lived much later than the above two, in the 13th century.

Having read all these stories, you may have some idea of what it takes to make a saint. Many saints are not canonised; some you will see bending over the kitchen sink or doing ordinary work quietly. The main thing is that the company of God does not make for sadness. All of these people were brave, and some faced appalling deaths cheerfully. On the other hand some lived without being noticed; there was the little princess named Edith who went into her convent at once and died at thirteen, but her life was so charitable she is called St. Edith of Wilton. 'She did not leave the world, she never knew it,' they said, as told in the article. Most of you will know the world, however. Do what you can in it for the sake of Christ, in whatever way you are asked to.

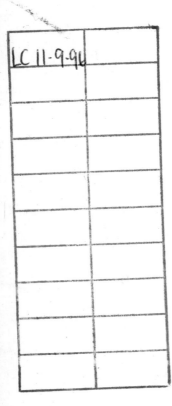

LC 11-9-96